HIRE
Performance

HIRE
Performance
RECRUITING A WINNING SALES TEAM
NEW AND REVISED

Dr. David K. Barnett
with Matthew Robinson

iUniverse LLC
Bloomington

HIRE PERFORMANCE
RECRUITING A WINNING SALES TEAM NEW AND REVISED

iUniverse books may be ordered through booksellers or by contacting:

iUniverse
1663 Liberty Drive
Bloomington, IN 47403
www.iuniverse.com
1-800-Authors (1-800-288-4677)

Because of the dynamic nature of the Internet, any web addresses or links contained in this book may have changed since publication and may no longer be valid. The views expressed in this work are solely those of the author and do not necessarily reflect the views of the publisher, and the publisher hereby disclaims any responsibility for them.

Any people depicted in stock imagery provided by Thinkstock are models, and such images are being used for illustrative purposes only.

Certain stock imagery © Thinkstock.

ISBN: 978-1-4759-9819-1 (sc)
ISBN: 978-1-4759-9820-7 (e)

Library of Congress Control Number: 2013912537

Printed in the United States of America.

iUniverse rev. date: 8/20/2013

CONTENTS

PREFACE TO THE SECOND EDITION

The first edition of this book succeeded beyond all of this author's expectations. It sold thousands of copies because it fills a very simple niche: it gives practical help to people tasked with recruiting and selecting salespeople. *Hire Performance: Recruiting a Winning Sales Team* was never intended to be a heavily footnoted scientific treatise for ivory-tower intellectuals but was a simple primer for frontline businesspeople tasked with finding, recruiting, and motivating sales teams. Many small and start-up businesses particularly need this help, because it often takes time for a company to grow sufficiently to permit specialized staffing. Until then the entrepreneur must wear many hats, among them HR manager and VP of sales. But few businesspeople have the time to educate themselves on equal opportunity laws and know little if anything beyond their own experience about sales, especially how to recruit a sales team. As important as sales is to the growth of any business, few MBA programs or business schools offer any training on the subject. Consequently entrepreneurs use themselves as the hiring template for recruiting, sometimes with disastrous consequences.

Since the book was first published in 2003, many business owners and quite a few HR professionals have written to say that the book was a valuable resource for understanding rudimentary mission-critical tasks, such as how to write a recruitment ad, where to look for the best candidates, how to evaluate employment assessments, and particularly, how to improve interview skills. My thanks to all those who wrote to say that they found the book helpful and many who shared new insights into the selection process that I am excited about incorporating into this second edition.

This edition contains several important changes to the first version of the book. The most noticeable update is that of the name of my coauthor, Matt Robinson. Matt has taken the theory behind this book to new levels, using its insights to take three separate sales organizations from worst to first. I've asked Matt to join me in writing the second edition so that we might provide you with the best information not only on the theory and research but on the practical application of this recruitment strategy we call *Hire Performance* to real-world management and recruiting.

Another change from the previous version of the book is the name of the sales assessment that we use in our research and as a tool for recruiters. You don't have to purchase SalesKey to gain from the theory we have built into the instrument. But we have continued to update our learning and to improve the tools we use.

There are four primary reasons we wrote this book. First, we heard from many entrepreneurs and start-up small-business owners who can't afford an entire HR department that the job they dreaded the most was trying to recruit salespeople. These businesspeople knew that developing a winning sales team was critical to the survival and success of their enterprise and that they couldn't afford to get it wrong. There has been so much misinformation about what makes a great salesperson that we wanted to weigh in on the subject with our research and the documented success we have had to help others build effective sales teams.

Second, some large companies that use our SalesKey assessment wanted a textbook to help their managers and recruiters leverage the assessment more effectively in both recruitment and the development of sales potential. But we want to be clear—you don't have to purchase SalesKey to profit from these pages.

Third, we have worked with many new clients since the first edition of this book and completed lots of new research that we wanted to share. We have not only worked in the United States but have broadened our experience to include Europe and Asia as well. Findings from those studies are included in this volume, although we won't bore you with a lot of statistical data.

Finally, not only do we know more than we did in 2003, but there's a whole new world of contact technologies that didn't exist a decade ago. We wanted to include new material on social media and its uses in sales recruiting. Additionally, sales keeps changing because young people are bringing a different worldview and new skills to the sales profession.

Matt Robinson and I are committed to continuous improvement of our assessments and training tools. Our goal is to create the most accurate, user-friendly programs available to small business owners, professional recruiters, and leaders of sales organizations around the world. To succeed we must welcome change and innovation. I can't wait for the third edition.

Dr. David K. Barnett

COAUTHOR'S PREFACE

In 1999 I happened to do a Yahoo search for sales assessments, and that one click permanently changed the direction of my life. More important, that one click and my subsequent association with Dr. Dave Barnett have changed the lives of thousands of people and their families over the past decade. This has largely been driven by a belief in two essential principles that underlie the approach we are going to use in this book. First, Hire Performance starts with an inherent belief in the capabilities that lie within each one of us. Dr. Dave told me that Hire Performance was different because it was rooted in the positive psychology movement. I had no idea what he was talking about then, but I've come to learn that this means that we don't want to put people in a box. Instead, Hire Performance wants to start with the gifts and aspirations of people to help them discover their fullest potential.

The second principle we have applied that has been truly unique has been a dedication to measure and develop behaviors that impact performance. There's not much in our approach about positive mental attitude and other subjective subjects. By focusing on what is real and measurable, we bypass the mind games to show salespeople an objective method to attain their goals. This has led to salespeople doubling their income in less than twelve months; going from being at the bottom of sales reports to the top within a year; helping people evolve from being dedicated service professionals to performing at top levels in high-income-earning sales jobs and watching as families reap the rewards of their fathers' and/or mothers' work.

I understand that you're probably a recruiter and not a trainer, like me. But I encourage you to do what I did: let this book introduce you to a different way of thinking about sales. Learn the model we present here. You will not only know more clearly what you're looking for when you need to hire salespeople but will also lay the groundwork for developing the talent you recruit to its fullest potential. Maybe you think you've hired the wrong person. You see some of your salespeople teetering on the verge of failure. Step back a moment and look at the folks you may have already hired in light of this new information and see how you can improve your recruiting as well as help current reps do better.

Thousands upon thousands of books on self-improvement and effective sales conversations have obviously been written, and yet never have I come across an approach as simple and effective as what you will see unfold in the pages that lie ahead. I urge you not to approach this as just another book to read and forget but rather as a diagnostic tool to what might be holding you as a sales rep or your team as a manager from its full potential. These pages contain a process proven over and over again to yield the same result: Hire Performance. Regardless of where you may sit today—at the top of your game or struggling to find success—you will find tactical suggestions on every page that will have an immediate impact on you and your team's success.

Matthew Robinson

INTRODUCTION
PREDICTING SALES PERFORMANCE

We are sales prognosticators who get paid to predict which potential employees will make money for a business and which will cost much more money to hire and train than they will ever generate. Over the years, we've gotten pretty good at it.

We've been challenged by companies in the United States and Europe to predict from a hodgepodge of employees which ones have become top-producing salespeople. They make it tough on us. Every salesperson they hired was positive, outgoing, and capable; not a ringer in the bunch. They were all good enough in face-to-face interviews to have persuaded experienced managers to hire them. But some had succeeded and others failed while many others teetered in the middle. Unlike their managers, I wasn't allowed to see or talk to any of these salespeople. What we had were SalesKey scores and reams of sales-production data. In that time SalesKey has proven to be approximately 80 percent accurate at differentiating top producers from mediocre ones. That success rate grows to over 90 percent when we predict those who will wash out of a sales career.

SalesKey is a sales core-competency profile developed in 1997 (the tool was called SalesMAP in those early days). Unlike the typical sales-personality test that makes huge inferences from a list of adjectives,

SalesKey measures stable traits—personality characteristics, behavior patterns, vocational interests, and skill competencies—associated with job performance in sales positions.

This book is about a recruiting system that minimizes intuition and subjective evaluation in favor of tools that provide more objective information about people. Hire Performance is not a product but is an approach to recruitment developed around Dr. Dave Barnett's Four Levels of Sales model. The Four Levels model sequences the skills of sales development; that is, it describes what candidates must bring with them to the job and the hierarchy of skills upon which sales success is built. One of the tools used in the approach is our SalesKey assessment for recruiters. SalesKey is convenient for many recruiters who want to use the Hire Performance system because the personal profile built from the assessment clearly identifies the elements of Barnett's model. This book is about what lies behind SalesKey and how you can use its insights to your advantage.

Hire Performance is a program that works. Companies putting into practice the principles outlined in this book have seen huge results.

- Charles Schwab saw a 173 percent increase in productivity in just three months, and this was at a time when the market was very unstable.
- Another brokerage house (we cannot use their name because they consider our service a competitive advantage and have sworn us to confidentiality) started hiring smarter and training their current reps in the behavioral model described in this book. Average rep gross income grew from $12,391 to $19,460 the following year—an increase of 37 percent. Over eighteen months, rep gross income increased 120 percent. Contacts tripled, and the value of the typical sale increased 27 percent. This same firm cut their turnover rate nearly in half within eighteen months.
- Henry Schein Dental saved more than $4.5 million *per year* when recruiters began using the Hire Performance system.
- In Europe, Pustelli, a multinational manufacturer, was concerned about a turnover rate approaching 70 percent.

Before implementing the Hire Performance system, they hired thirty salespeople and found that six months later, only ten were still on the payroll. After implementing this system of hiring by behavioral analysis, they found that twenty-five of the twenty-eight reps hired in the preceding year were still with the company, and sales were higher than they had ever been.

While these case studies are notable, they are not unusual. In one study done with Campbell's Soup, we tracked a return on investment of 8,623 percent (that's not a typo) for every dollar invested in our assessments and training.

This book contains what we've learned from years of extensive research into sales productivity and the actual practice of hiring salespeople. We've condensed nearly five decades of combined sales and sales-management experience into a turnkey system you can use to improve your odds at hiring top sales talent.

This book has three main parts:

1. The Basics
2. The Four Levels of Sales
3. Level Four Behaviors for Recruiters

The Basics begins with a discussion of the scientific basis for our approach. We believe in quantifying things, because selling is a quantifiable occupation. In chapters 1 and 2, we develop a view of sales as science rather than as primarily a subjective art. We hope to encourage you in chapter 3 to confront something on which we have become quite expert—contact hesitation in salespeople. We provide you with a checklist and a self-scoring system to determine whether you suffer from contact hesitation, and if so, to possibly pinpoint some of the root causes. The Basics includes the fact that recruiting is selling. In chapter 4 we argue that it's a strategic type of sale that builds on the power of relationships and not just transactions.

The second part of book looks at how salespeople develop from rookies into superstars. We call this path *the Four Levels of Sales*. We base our SalesKey assessment and our Hire Performance selection system around this model, which helps us know what to look for in salespeople and provides a sequence of skills that we can use to anticipate future problems. Each level is made up of behaviors. In chapter 6 we introduce you to six foundational behaviors necessary to perform the essential tasks of any sales position that we call Level 1. Chapter 7 focuses on two Level 2 behaviors: focus and problem solving. In chapter 8 we introduce some of the strengths and challenges of current models for understanding behaviors that are popular in business and show how our model incorporates the strengths of each while minimizing drawbacks. Level 3 is made up of four emotional needs, which we detail in chapter 9 before looking at the impact of each emotional need on teamwork and compatibility in chapter 10.

The last part of the book develops seven specific Level 4 skills for recruiters to practice in their drive to exceed expectations. In chapter 12 we spell out how to leverage a comp plan to maximize productivity. Chapter 13 focuses on where recruiters should look for qualified candidates. Building on the Four Levels of Sales model, chapter 14 discusses how to write job ads that target more specifically the people you want to reach with your opportunity. Next we discuss how to evaluate résumés and use social media to unearth the information you need. Chapter 17 lays out some tips for having a great first interview. Since most recruiters use sales-hiring tests after the initial interview, we devote chapters 18 and 19 to sales-selection assessments. Chapter 20 is an extensive treatment of behavioral interviewing, including sample questions for the seventeen critical behaviors discussed in the Four Levels section. We conclude with chapter 21 on negotiation, and chapter 22 summarizes the program.

Your title might be sales manager, VP of sales, HR manager, or entrepreneur, or you might work for a recruiting firm, but to make this book easier to read, we will refer to people who make decisions about hiring salespeople as recruiters.

Hire Performance gets results. Master a few key skills and we can predict that your company will reap great rewards not only in the short term but for a long time to come.

1

IS SALES ART OR SCIENCE?

Let's start at the beginning, zeroing in on the question "Is sales art or science?" Believe it or not, knowing the difference has a profound impact on how you approach recruiting. One common problem shared by many companies struggling to grow sales is that so few have developed objective, scientific metrics for evaluating success. Yes, they all look for bottom-line financial results. But many sales organizations and HR departments are clueless about how those results happen.

Take the example of Company A, who engaged us to test their salespeople and build a hiring template that would help them detect and measure the skills and aptitudes of their top performers. Their reps were territory managers. When we asked for corporate sales data, we discovered that Company A only tracks the sales of a territory, not the individual salesperson. It had never occurred to them to subtract the sales from previous territory reps to determine how well the current salesperson was actually doing. The situation was made even worse when we tried to explain the problem. As we talked about the behaviors that actually drive results, shoulders shrugged and eyes glazed over.

When we begin work with a client, we typically do a research study in which we compare SalesKey scores to the actual productivity of salespeople. That way we can correlate which specific behaviors differentiate top performers from mediocre ones. In a project for a major hospital chain, they had no metrics. A major credit card organization had no metrics. When asked how they evaluated productivity, the senior managers told us they didn't. As it turned out, their turnover rates were so high that nobody stayed around long enough to develop success measures.

Thomas Dolby had a song on the charts some time back called "She Blinded Me with Science." The lyrics probably confused a lot of us born in the first half of the twentieth century. We thought science was supposed to give us clarity. How could science blind anybody?

CULTURE SHIFT

Growing up we used to look forward to getting *My Weekly Reader*, a publication for kids filled with the latest scientific discoveries and stories about how new gadgets were going to make life easier and better in the future. Baby boomers (people born between 1946 and 1964) were pretty much brainwashed by education and pop culture to be cockeyed optimists. They were value-programmed to believe that everything was just going to get better and better. In junior high and high school, the boomers sat in rapt attention listening to countdowns from Cape Canaveral over school public address systems. Science was going to save the world.

Then came the turbulent 1960s. Some went to college, while others went to fight and die in Vietnam. In college, intellectuals taught that science had blinded us to tragedy, that we were naïve to trust science. Science and technology didn't produce utopia; they brought us Hiroshima and Auschwitz. Create the Internet and what do you get? Pornography, spam, identity theft, and much worse. The next generation, sometimes called Gen Xers, rebelled against their parents' optimism and went so far as to reject the very idea that something was either true or false. When a person believes that all ideas possess moral equivalence and truth is relative, the result is cynicism. The cynics said the scientist always has an agenda. This new philosophy of universal skepticism came to be known as postmodernism.

Postmodernism has completely infected public education, religion, and media pop culture. There's always been dishonesty, but cheating is on the rise in education, politics, and business. The new ethic seems to be "It's only wrong if you get caught." Good and evil are relative. One country's terrorist is another's freedom fighter. The culture has become more and more litigious because contracts are just words, and words are meaningless. News programs no longer report what happened but what polls or pundits say might happen. Spirituality is back in vogue (as long as it's not part of any organized religion). Reality is subjective.

This postmodern worldview has had a profound impact on business and especially sales. Objective measurements are not only being discarded but are claimed to be detrimental to corporate sales culture. Sales productivity is no longer merely about results but about happiness and having fun. The postmodern sales mantra is simple: selling is all about relationships. People looking for sales jobs today appear to be less money-motivated. Many regard their jobs the way their grandparents probably felt about church or synagogue—a place to meet people and provide meaning for their lives. Sales managers and recruiters in the twenty-first century are less likely to know anything about the science of sales but hold strong opinions about selling that they are convinced are true. If you can avoid objective behavioral standards, you can avoid any pressure to improve performance. What counts in postmodern business is feeling good about oneself in spite of lackluster effort. Most sales training doesn't work, because sales teams are populated with unproductive reps who have never been told that they are wrong or off-target in their life and who only expect coaching and mentoring from managers around issues of self-esteem rather than productivity. Because managers are oblivious to how to fix the problems of sales productivity, they draft mission statements and do their 360 surveys (was there ever a more postmodern concept of truth than the 360 evaluation?).

Believing at some preconscious level that science can't be entirely trusted, companies have bought into sales recruitment and development solutions based on what can only be described as mysticism and alchemy; the belief that we can detect metaphysical properties that allow us to make any reality we choose; that if you can conceive and believe, you can achieve, as one modern sorcerer claims. If company profits are falling, we stop measuring the bottom line and measure something else—perhaps quality or teamwork or customer satisfaction—because we have to feel good about ourselves. Reality is whatever we make it.

"We've won the Malcolm Baldridge Award five years running," one VP of sales told Dr. Barnett quite proudly.

"But the company has had four years of declining sales," Barnett said. "What about that?"

"We believe customer satisfaction is what counts," he said, showing the good doctor to the door.

The following year the business was bought out and effectively dismantled, leaving the VP of sales looking for a new job.

Businesses invest millions to learn the mantras of a whole new generation of consultants who combine ancient secrets with modern science to produce such postmodern topics as Feng Shui Sales Force, Discovering the Sales Secrets of Attila the Hun (or Sun Tzu or some other dead potentate), or How Meditation Can Make You a Millionaire.

SUBJECTIVE VS. OBJECTIVE

Postmodern businesspeople focus on the art of selling. Science seems cold and impersonal. In one experiment that spanned more than a decade, we asked over four hundred sales managers and recruiters to create a simple list of behaviors that make a successful salesperson. There were almost as many different answers as there were people answering the question. But 97 percent of the answers had one thing in common: they were subjective and not objective terms. The most frequent answer was that sales success required "persistence." Other attributes in the top ten included "positive attitude," "belief in what they sell," "self-confidence," "strong product knowledge," "integrity," and other words one might find in the glossary of any self-help book. These are mental and emotional constructs open to interpretation, unlike fact-based attributes, such as "making twenty prospecting sales calls per day," "meeting or exceeding sales targets," or "asking questions."

This evidence suggests that most recruiters have been unwittingly brainwashed to think of successful salesmanship as something almost entirely subjective; as art outside the realm of science. If selling is metaphysical, companies should hire shamans and spiritualists, and many do.

One enormous problem with relying on subjective measures of success is that you never know when you have succeeded. Without objective benchmarks, it's all open to interpretation. One rep's perseverance may be another's stubbornness. How does a recruiter know if one salesperson's attitude is more positive than another? How do you measure belief? Subjective definitions are fleeting fashions that can change from day to day, from minute to minute. How can we quantify the ephemeral in any meaningful way?

Please do not misunderstand. We are not saying that there is no art to selling. Sales craft is highly creative. But like any artist, you cannot practice the art without first mastering basic skills and knowledge. Architects design form to follow function. They work with the science of physics before they can responsibly tackle the aesthetics of design. Although some artists can literally throw paint on a canvas, give it a name, and find people gullible enough to pay for it, this is not a sustainable business without someone who understands the psychology of media and the sociology of marketing. Musicians must know music theory, or else their improvisations soon become predictable.

Talk of the art of sales is most appropriate when discussing the conversation of the salesperson with a customer or prospect. Creativity, nuance, and style make sales uniquely expressive. But before one can practice the art of conversation, the salesperson must have someone to talk to. What good is the ability to carry on an engaging sales conversation if salespeople don't get in front of enough prospects to reach their sales goals? Here's a Hire Performance foundational principle: in sales, science precedes art. The salesperson earns the right to create art by paying attention to the science.

This principle holds true for recruiters and hiring managers tasked with building a sales team. Most managers enjoy the sophisticated analysis of personality and high-level conversation so much more than the grind-it-out practicality of writing ads, reading résumés, and doing those initial phone interviews. The subjective art of sales is rewarding and enjoyable precisely because there no accountability for art. Something "means" whatever the artist wants it to mean. But science is a taskmaster, insisting on inconvenient facts and keeping score.

QUANTITATIVE SELLING

The wonderful thing about a sales career is that selling conforms to the laws of large numbers. Its probabilities are exact. A salesperson who knows his sales science can predict exactly how much he or she is going to earn, and although that rep may not be able to point out which prospect will buy and which will not, the outcome is statistically certain. In study after study, we confirm the basic premise that the best predictor of sales success is not the personality of the rep or the reputation of the company but the size of the pipeline the salesperson builds, a pipeline that contains the most number of people all at different stages in the sales process. If a salesperson talks to twenty prospects, we can predict the number of sales made. Getting back to objective numbers puts us back on the most stable ground imaginable for improving our productivity. This is why Hire Performance looks at objective metrics, rooting recruitment in time-honored methodologies from a time before gurus and theoreticians with their postmodern MBAs began remaking sales in the image of self-help psychology.

CONCLUSION

Selling has evolved in our society into something less quantitative and more subjective. Hire Performance is a back-to-basics approach, emphasizing that measurable facts come before the abstract and subjective art of sales. Since selling conforms so well to the laws of probability, managers should use sales science to improve productivity. The science of sales makes recruiting a winning sales team a lot easier and more manageable.

2

OBSERVE, MEASURE, AND REPEAT

Let's apply some science to recruiting a winning sales team. We need to find elements of the recruitment process that can be quantified rather than left open to subjective interpretation. The whole point of science is to determine what can be analyzed, standardized, and then repeated time and time again with regularity to produce an outcome we desire. Because we are dealing with fallible human beings, this process will never be perfect because we can never completely eliminate human assumption and error. But we can get a lot closer to success if we intentionally follow a simple three-step process: Observe. Measure. Repeat.

STEP 1: OBSERVE

It's critical that the recruiter watch salespeople in their environment. If you work for a larger company, consider going on sales calls with your existing top people and also your struggling reps. If you're starting a new company, ask sales managers in your industry if you can watch their salespeople. Learn as much as you can firsthand. Recruiters of winning sales teams must know what differentiates successful salespeople from those who fail. Even more important, recruiters should pay close attention to the behaviors and skills that distinguish top performers from the merely mediocre. It's not always easy to spot these behavioral difference makers. To do so, you must not only look at the superstars. You have to observe the also-rans too.

We asked the owners of a real estate company what they thought differentiated their top producers from their struggling reps. They said top salespeople were more "positive" and more "outgoing." However, when we assessed their sales team, we found that the weakest producers were just as optimistic and outgoing as the top producers. Both groups had excellent product knowledge, and all went through exactly the same sales-training program. The real differentiator, it turned out, was nothing in their personality at all. It was the number of attempted contacts made per day. The close ratio between top real estate reps and mediocre ones was identical, about one close in every three presentations. But top producers averaged about thirty attempted contacts per day while the poor performers averaged less than half that many. The true difference between top and bottom performers did not become apparent until we observed what the salespeople actually did on a daily basis.

These observed activities are the verifiable success competencies in your selling environment. There's nothing wrong with looking for people with perseverance. We want to emphasize that you clarify for yourself what are the specific behaviors that allow you to know your candidate will persevere. It's not enough to ask, "Are you persevering?" and hear your applicant say, "Yes." What are the behavioral clues that objectify a characteristic? For example, does she make more sales calls than other people? Work longer hours? Or does he complain less about missed opportunities? What will you observe that will quantify your conclusion? Perhaps you're looking for candidates who display a positive mental attitude. What is the marker behavior that signals optimism in salespeople? What does it look like? Do these people smile more? Do they give more compliments? Learn to observe behaviors that differentiate top performers from weak performers.

Some high-priced consultants claim that they can save you the trouble of observing salespeople by equipping you with ready-made lists of "competencies" accumulated from other businesses "just like yours." Be cautious with these so-called competencies. Many could be nonquantifiable mental states or feelings.

One management-consultant company lists the following as sales competencies:

- has written goals
- follows sales plan
- has positive outlook
- takes responsibility
- strong self-confidence
- supportive beliefs
- controls emotions

How many of these characteristics would you say are observable and quantifiable? Perhaps one or two, but the rest are subjective and beyond the ability of the typical sales recruiter to quantify. When we say quantifiable, we mean, "Did you see this behavior or not?" or "Can this be verified objectively?" I can perhaps quantify item #1 as true if the individual shows me a list of goals to be achieved with time frames. But what metrics are there for the rest of the items? How do I know if someone has a positive outlook? Is strong self-confidence something you do (behavior) or something you are (characteristic)? The further from objective behavior we get, the more difficult it becomes to quantify.

In addition to evaluating whether a competency is objective or subjective, it helps to know if it connects in any meaningful way to the sales process. How many of the seven competencies above would you say relate directly to increasing sales? Perhaps #2, Follows Sales Plans, but even that is vague. Is it just us or do most of these "competencies" have more to do with finding salespeople who will be easy to manage rather than salespeople who will drive bottom-line sales?

So what kind of behavioral competencies would qualify as contributing directly to sales? Terminology may differ from company to company, but here's a preliminary list that can apply to most sales positions.

- attempted phone dials
- attempted contacts
- handing out business cards (sometimes called "meet and greet")

- conversations
- set and kept appointments
- presentations
- attempted closes
- closed sales
- follow-up contacts

These behaviors are quantifiable. They either happen or they don't. Each is critical to almost any sales process and therefore contributes directly to the bottom line. You can probably add other behaviors that apply to the product or service you sell. This list isn't exhaustive, but it is meant to be suggestive of the kinds of activities for which the professional recruiter and sales manager looks.

If you are a recruiter who does not or cannot observe salespeople, you can practice what business guru Tom Peters calls "management by walking around." There is no substitute for listening to phone reps conversing with different types of customers, riding with outside reps as they make their calls, and visiting with their managers to drill down to the bedrock of behavioral excellence. If you don't yet have salespeople on the payroll, ask a friend who works in a similar sales position to yours if you can shadow him or her for a day or two. Many salespeople will be flattered to act as a mentor. If someone hesitates, offer to pay $500 for the privilege. It will be well worth it.

STEP 2: MEASURE

Next you must know how many times salespeople need to perform the behaviors you observed in Step 1 in order to reach their sales goals. You must measure the behaviors. It's not enough to know what top producers do. You must also measure how often they do it.

Lorenzo is a recruiter in the life insurance business. Making prospecting telephone calls to referred leads is a critical behavior for success in his market. Lorenzo knows that if he asks, "Can you ask for referrals?" most candidates respond enthusiastically in the affirmative.

"Asking 'Can you?' is the wrong question," Lorenzo explains. "They all say they can, but will they? That's the money question."

Lorenzo has measured the performance of his top performers and knows that they ask for referrals about twenty times a week. Poor performers, in spite of completing the company's "Sixteen Ways to Ask for Referrals" class, ask fewer than three people per week for referrals. Armed with this objective data, Lorenzo increases his odds of recruiting a winning sales team significantly when he asks, "How many referrals do you get each week?"

Lorenzo knows exactly what he's looking for—someone who has a proven track record of asking for a minimum of fifteen to twenty referrals weekly. Specific measurements characterize top performers. Winners keep score.

In order to know which job seeker is best for your sales position, you should not only gauge the presence of a particular behavior but determine if the individual has experience performing that particular behavior enough times to succeed in your enterprise. For example, you need someone who is at ease meeting strangers. You observe that your candidate seems very poised meeting you for the first time. But meeting one or two people with poise is relatively easy, especially if he's trying to perform well to get a job. So quantify the success behavior by finding out how many new people he meets each day in his current position. This leads us to the third element of Hire Performance.

STEP 3: REPEAT

In addition to being measurable, success factors you observe and count must also be repeatable. Lorenzo has a system. He doesn't continually change his approach because he gets emotionally attached to a candidate who doesn't quite fit the template he's designed. As a Hire Performance recruiter, you have to be consistent in applying your selection criteria. You standardize the hiring process. Employment law pretty much requires that you put everybody through the same routine. Now, that isn't always possible. But the point we want to make is to be very wary of abandoning your recruitment system in the search for an exception to the rule.

Take Larnelle for example. He's a veteran sales manager for a financial services firm for which we developed a customized selection template.

We gave SalesKey to more than three hundred of the firm's salespeople, correlated test scores with actual dollars-and-cents production, and came up with a cut-off score based on how nearly their profile matched a benchmark. We had conclusively demonstrated that the chances of hiring an above-average performer was more than 80 percent if that candidate scored ten or more points on this selection scale.

Larnelle was down two full-time positions in his branch. He was under pressure to fill those seats. This was during a time when jobs were not scarce and financial markets were booming. After receiving fewer résumés than he had expected, Larnelle finally found two salespeople who wanted the job. Larnelle gave each the SalesKey assessment as prescribed by the company's hiring policy. When the results came back, one of the reps scored eleven points on the selection score, but the other scored only four points.

Larnelle ignored the SalesKey profile and hired both individuals. The company allowed a recruiter to override the assessment selection score if there were extenuating circumstances. In Larnelle's case, he just had a great feeling about these two sales reps. He refused to believe what the assessment was saying about Jason, the rep who only scored four points. Larnelle argued that the assessment was wrong, because Jason had done so well at his previous employer selling the same financial services as Larnelle's company. The truth is that Larnelle wasn't open to getting objective, scientific information. He had already hired Jason in his mind; he wanted Jason to fit, regardless of the science involved.

As it turned out, Jason was terminated six months later for poor production. Larnelle didn't know that Jason's last sales job was that of an account manager with a fixed clientele. He didn't have to prospect, and he didn't have to initiate sales calls, which were critical to success at Larnelle's company.

Candidates put their best foot forward, pretending to be something they're not in hopes of confounding the system; recruiters inject their biases and prejudices into the selection process to give some preferential treatment. The system built to capitalize on the scientific laws of repetition is negated. Science dissolves into intuition, and objectivity is lost.

Does this mean that you should never update your system or change your selection process? Of course not. Economic shifts can cause fluctuations in the marketplace. Sometimes it's an employer's market, and sometimes it's a job-seeker's market. You have to build your scientific strategy in light of the measurable observations you have at the moment. But times change. Keep alert to the shifts in your industry. Don't stop talking to other people who do what you do. Keep observing. Keep measuring. When something changes, update your recruiting system accordingly. But sometimes pressures will exist to hire someone who isn't ideal. Clue in the front-line manager early on to the strengths and weaknesses of a candidate. Be specific about your observations. Have the manager build in some repetition of training where there may be a weakness in the candidate's skill level. Hire Performance is not a ball and chain to which you are bound but a carefully constructed process that can help you get it right in good times and hedge your bets in tough times.

CONCLUSION

Sales science requires that you:

- Observe the behaviors that are most effective for producing sales. Don't focus on subjective characteristics. Watch both low and high performers.
- Measure the number of times top performers do these behaviors. If you can't observe them, they aren't measurable.
- Repeat your system with each candidate. Be alert to the pressures that can compromise your objectivity. Revise your system only in the light of new observations and measurements.

3

CONFRONTING RECRUITMENT RELUCTANCE

The greatest enemy of the recruiter designing and then sticking with a system built around objective metrics is something called *recruitment reluctance*. If recruiting isn't your only duty and you're uncomfortable with recruiting, you're not alone. Our research with sales organizations suggests that as many as 60 percent of managers are uncomfortable with some aspect of recruiting. Approximately half of these recruitment-reluctant managers are so discouraged that they are actively planning to leave their current position in search of a less emotionally demanding career.

We don't want to add to your guilt or discomfort if you don't particularly like recruiting. Recruiters are on the hot seat every day to produce results. We want to show you how the antidote to emotional burnout is found in knowing the predictable science that underlies your task. The more objective the process becomes, the less likely you're going to expend emotional resources coping with it. Depending on your personality, you may never feel like a natural-born recruiter, but that doesn't mean that you can't build a solid sales organization through a dependable process.

Although we've tried to be thorough, we probably won't be able to answer every question you could ever ask about sales recruitment. Whenever you deal with people, it's impossible to perfectly predict every situation and need. But if you're new to recruiting, we can help get you up and running, or at least headed in the right direction, as quickly as possible. If you're an experienced recruiter, Hire Performance will make you even better with creative new ideas and research-based solutions to some of your greatest challenges.

RECRUITING IS SELLING

For those charged with recruiting a winning sales team, hiring is a sales manager's most important duty. Nothing is more critical than getting good people on your sales team—not paperwork, not analysis, not corporate politics, not motivating the troops, nothing. These additional responsibilities of management are necessary, but they are essentially meaningless if the front-line recruiter can't put together and keep together a top-quality sales team.

There are as many myths about what makes a great recruiter as there are about what makes a successful salesperson. But it turns out that everything we've learned about top sales performers also applies to top-gun recruiters, because recruiting is selling.

Recruiting may be the toughest sales job of all. Why? First, recruiters must sell some of the very best salespeople. It's easy to feel intimidated. Although many salespeople are impulse buyers, the higher-paid reps are frequently more experienced and more analytical. They ask tough questions. They can negotiate well. The recruiter who hesitates or stumbles with these communication pros can come across as uncertain and leave a negative impression with a strong candidate.

Another reason recruiting can be difficult is because the recruiter must sell an intangible benefit. It's always easier to sell a commodity for less than someone else. As much as some recruiters may reduce the process to a matter of how much the job pays, top-quality salespeople want to reap many other benefits in addition to compensation. Will the manager they are working for develop their talent? Is the company stable enough to offer a long-term commitment? What are the chances for promotion? Recruiters sell the intangible benefit that a specific opportunity or company will satisfy the emotional needs of the sales professional.

So selling salespeople can be a tough job. But the primary reason recruiters don't make more money by making more quality placements is because they don't talk to enough people. Recruiters struggle and frequently fail for the same reasons salespeople fail—they don't leverage the science to know how many contacts lead to how many conversations lead to how many appointments lead to how many hires. If you're a struggling recruiter, is it because you have a lousy personality or you aren't thinking enough positive thoughts? Or is the problem that you allow yourself to be distracted by all the other things that need doing so that you can avoid what is emotionally unpleasant for you—selling to salespeople? Mediocre recruiters, like poor-performing salespeople, spend more time, energy, and resources coping with their own emotional barriers to recruiting than being engaged in the actual behaviors of recruiting. Some get more wrapped up in administration than making calls. Others would rather hold meetings than get out of their offices to attend a job fair or put themselves in front of highly qualified candidates. Still others allow rearranging files to take precedence over following up leads. It may be that office politics and gossip are more pleasurable pursuits than getting referrals.

RECRUITMENT RELUCTANCE

Recruitment reluctance refers to all the barriers recruiters develop to initiating contacts with potential and current clients. Customer contact is the core competency of all sales jobs, and that includes being a recruiter. It's impossible to make a sale if you haven't connected with a potential customer. Sales don't mysteriously appear from heaven. Business must be developed by conscious effort. Products and services can be promoted in many ways—print, broadcast media, Internet, word-of-mouth. But the universal, irreducible, subatomic activity in every sales situation is the person-to-person contact. Sellers must find and interact with buyers.

As a middleman, recruiters must create demand as well as fulfill the demand. They sell in two directions simultaneously. In order to find candidates, sales managers must develop extensive networks of people and organizations as sources of referrals and lead generation. They must also work with employers able and willing to pay for their service. While independent recruiters and headhunters know the importance of prospecting employers, in-house sales managers frequently overlook this prospect pool. Sales managers in a company may not call other businesses, but they must identify and learn to satisfy internal customers, the people in the organization who depend on the recruiters doing the best possible job. Everyone who has a stake in generating more profit for the business is an internal customer for the sales recruiter. Top-notch manager-recruiters make lots of contacts with the people in the organization who can make a difference in what the manager earns.

Good recruiters, like great salespeople, make lots of contacts with the right people. Who are the "right people"? Anyone who can make a difference in what I earn. Those who struggle with recruitment reluctance don't see enough candidates or promote themselves effectively within the organization. Recruitment reluctance blinds managers and recruiters to the contact dependency of their work.

If you want to build a winning sales team, begin by looking at yourself. Here's a quick do-it-yourself diagnostic of your recruiting aptitude. Please answer these questions as honestly as you can allow yourself to be. The more candid your answers, the more likely you will benefit from this exercise.

RECRUITING PERFORMANCE CHECKLIST

Circle the answer that comes closest to describing your answer to each of the following items.

1. Within my industry, I would evaluate my current recruitment efforts to be:
    1. Far below average
    2. Somewhat below average
    3. About average
    4. Somewhat above average
    5. Far above average

2. When I was in sales, I considered prospecting a necessary evil.
   1. True
   2. I was never in sales, but I would have probably not enjoyed prospecting as much as other aspects of selling.
   3. I was never in sales, so I'm not certain how I would have felt about prospecting.
   4. I was never in sales, but I believe I would have devoted a great deal of energy to prospecting.
   5. False

3. In our sales organization, we prefer to use another term (for example, "account executive," "consultant," etc.) less offensive than "salesperson."
   1. Very true
   2. Somewhat true
   3. Uncertain
   4. Somewhat false
   5. Very false

4. I probably worry more than most recruiters about whether my reps are going to make it in our sales organization.
   1. Very true
   2. Somewhat true
   3. Uncertain
   4. Somewhat false
   5. Very false

5. I've been successful recruiting a certain way, and I'm not likely to change it now.
   1. Very true
   2. Somewhat true
   3. Uncertain
   4. Somewhat false
   5. Very false

6. I'm a bottom-line person who doesn't need to spend a lot of time analyzing situations.
   1. Very true
   2. Somewhat true
   3. Uncertain
   4. Somewhat false
   5. Very false

7. As a sales manager, what priority do you give to helping salespeople feel good about their career choice?
   1. Very high; one of my top priorities
   2. Somewhat high; probably in top ten
   3. Uncertain
   4. Somewhat low; something to talk about once in a while
   5. Very little, if any

8. When recruiting, I expect salespeople to show initiative by calling me rather than me calling candidates.
   1. Very true
   2. Somewhat true
   3. Uncertain
   4. Somewhat false
   5. Very false

9. I could do a better job at recruiting if I had been given proper training.
   1. Very true
   2. Somewhat true
   3. Uncertain
   4. Somewhat false
   5. Very false

10. Right now, I would estimate that about _____ of my time is spent every day in administrative tasks and meetings that prevent me from talking to as many recruits as I could/should.
   1. 80 percent or more
   2. Two-thirds
   3. Uncertain
   4. Half
   5. A third or less

HOW TO SCORE YOUR CHECKLIST

To determine your recruiting performance score, add up the numbers of your answers on each of the ten questions. If you answered every question by circling #5, your score would be 50 (5 x 10). If you circled #1 on every item, you would have the minimum score of 10.

My Score: _____

Use the following information to interpret your score.

Score	Interpretation
10–30	You appear to have chronic recruitment reluctance that could be significantly limiting your effectiveness.
31–40	You appear to have some recruitment reluctance that may be limiting your effectiveness.
41–50	Congratulations! You appear to be a Hire Performer! Very little recruitment reluctance indicated.

Special Note to Hire Performers: The fact that you have scored well on this checklist doesn't mean that you should give up reading this book. If you're like most top recruiters, you'll be looking for every way possible to improve your performance. If you scored above 40 and are feeling somewhat content with your recruiting efforts, deduct 20 points from your score, as you are obviously reluctant and looking for any excuse to do less.

FOUR CAUSES OF RECRUITMENT RELUCTANCE

Nobody is born a recruiter. Recruiting is a skill set that is learned. Good recruiters are not identified by any single personality trait or management style. Effective team-builders aren't all glad-handing, self-confident extroverts. Outgoing social types may have instincts that drive them intuitively to do certain things that improve their recruiting efficiency, but these are behaviors anyone can learn with practice. You can begin to overcome your recruitment reluctance by 1) learning and practicing a few basic behaviors and skills; and 2) investing in the tools needed to become a "Hire Performer."

What makes a manager reluctant to recruit? There are probably many causes, but here are four of the most common origins.

1. Contact Hesitation

Many recruiters suffer a common malady found among salespeople—contact hesitation. Contact hesitation (CH) is characterized by self-imposed limits on prospecting and client contact. CH is driven by internal needs that make avoiding people more emotionally satisfying than contacting people. Some reps and recruiters avoid talking to the very people who can increase their productivity and income (prospective new clients). People with CH don't make enough calls—and they know it! In severe cases, those with CH don't prospect at all. Like battle fatigue, the recruiter stares at the phone and shuffles prospect lists. Questions #2 and #8 on the checklist diagnose contact hesitation issues.

Contact hesitation is an emotional handicap that afflicts veteran as well as novice salespeople. Novices endure prospecting. Dr. Barnett remembers a sales manager telling him when he started in one sales job, "You'll have to do a lot of prospecting at first, but when you succeed you won't have to do that anymore."

"I believed it," Barnett says. "I built a very successful book of business, and then I stopped prospecting. That's when the business stopped growing."

He did what a lot of novice reps do—suffered through hundreds of prospecting cold calls, eagerly fantasizing about the day when he wouldn't have to put up with this "necessary evil." It wasn't until years later that Dr. Barnett finally understood this experience as one of the influences that created his contact hesitation.

Sales veterans frequently stop prospecting as soon as they develop enough key accounts to maintain a comfort zone. That's when sales productivity begins to plateau. It has nothing to do with not believing in the product or being motivated to succeed. CH develops when good reps hit that point at which they are convinced prospecting is no longer necessary and somewhat beneath their dignity.

The cost of contact hesitation in a recruiting manager is much greater to the organization than it is in an individual salesperson. The reluctant manager not only impacts his or her own career performance but, as our early sales experience showed, also infects members of the entire sales team with pernicious attitudes and productivity-stopping behaviors.

The cure for contact hesitation is accountability for working your sales science in the achievement of a personal goal. You must identify something that is meaningful to you that is worth your labor and potential struggle. It must be a goal that motivates you. It should be a goal that has a price tag. By that we don't necessarily mean it has to be something you buy, but you should identify the cost of attaining a nonmaterial goal. For example, you may want to go to Europe and study being a chef. You must calculate how much it will cost you to live and attend school and be unemployed for how many months while you learn to cook and until you can get a job that satisfies you. All this costs money. So get the price tag for your motivating goal. Keep it constantly in front of you. Then use your sales science to plot the daily activities that achieve that goal. If it's going to cost you $100,000 to become a French sous chef and you know your average commission is $1,000 per recruit, you know you have to place one hundred recruits. Then if you know your success ratio, you break your big goal down into the daily goals you need to achieve. If last year you placed 80 people and made 100 contacts per day (dials, messages left, etc.), then if you increase your contacts by 20 percent to 120 contacts per day, your goal can be achieved.

As long as you can identify a goal that is worth the struggle, you can overcome contact hesitation.

2. Poor Sales Identity

Some recruiters are refugees from a sales career. They put in their time in the front lines, and when the chance came to escape the daily grind of sales, they grabbed it. These managers won't admit it, and some aren't even aware of it, but they didn't enjoy sales. They "endured" and "paid their dues" to get promoted to a "real" job. This overt or covert negative attitude toward selling leads to another source of recruitment reluctance—poor sales identity.

Sales managers with poor sales identity will not be effective recruiters of sales talent. Ambivalent feelings about selling make recruiting psychologically painful as the manager struggles to enlist others in a career he or she was happy to have escaped. Managers with poor sales identity often don't like salespeople. They distrust them and uncritically accept negative stereotypes of salespeople. Recruiters with a poor sales identity may develop an us-vs.-them mentality, assuming reps are dishonest, lazy, or not very intelligent. It's not hard to see how such cynicism could impede recruiting.

Question #3 on the checklist identifies one telltale sign of sales identity issues. Recruiters with poor sales identity create and value pseudo-titles for salespeople, like "consultant" or "relationship manager." They use these alternative terms to soften what they perceive to be the negative impact of having a job in sales. When organizations sanction pseudo-titles, managers and recruiters are subtly brainwashed into thinking that sales is something of which salespeople should be ashamed. New employees may not have sales identity issues when they arrive at such an organization, but they are likely to develop sales prejudices soon thereafter.

Question #7 diagnoses sales identity concerns by asking you to rank the priority you think should be given to helping salespeople feel good about their career choice. Recruiters with poor sales identity invariably rank the issue higher than managers who have been in sales themselves for a period of time. Motivational hype can be another carrier of poor sales identity throughout an organization. Having salespeople shout, "I love selling!" at a pep rally may satisfy the anxieties of upper management, but it rarely accomplishes anything more than making reps wonder why so much energy is invested in such theatrics. Maybe it's because recruitment-reluctant leaders and managers don't really believe that selling is an honorable career choice.

When we first went to work with Charles Schwab, the company suffered from what can only be described as horrible sales identity. On a scale of 1–100 with 100 representing solid sales identity, the average SalesKey sales-identity score for both reps and managers was only slightly over 20. In those days, "sales" was actually considered a dirty word at Schwab. We asked one of the senior managers who was a close personal friend of Mr. Schwab himself to ask him how far he would have gotten in those early days if he didn't "sell." A few days later in a company-wide phone call, the great man affirmed that he had always been a great salesperson and that selling was an honorable and noble profession. He explained that he may have gone too far in his stereotyping of salespeople as being pushy and rude. By taking the lead, Charles Schwab enabled his firm to develop a more positive view of selling and better differentiate themselves from the competition. It was a sea change in the culture of the company. Sales became a word associated with pride and not shame. It's no surprise that the results posted by the sales teams of both companies shot up like a rocket during this same twelve-month period.

A positive sales identity begins at the top. The organization will take your lead and hire solid people who love their work, creating a positive corporate sales culture, and the results will follow.

3. Poor Risk Management

Another cause of recruitment reluctance is poor risk management. Hiring is risky business. Accountants make lousy recruiters because they let the risk of a hiring mistake dictate an excessively cautious strategy. Hiring mistakes can be very costly. One sales director for Campbell's Soup told me that it cost the firm $220,000 every time he hired a sales dud.

"Some mistakes I can undo or cover up," he said, "but my butt's on the line if I hire the wrong person."

Whether you're a hiring rookie or veteran recruiter, it's easy to feel intimidated by the need to manage the risk of a bad sales hire. If pressure doesn't arise from inside you, you may feel external pressure from the organization to get it right.

Problems occur when recruiters try to *over*manage the risk by becoming cautious in the extreme. Obsessive worry is the signature behavior of poor risk management (see question #4). Risk-averse recruiters drive up hiring costs by overanalyzing and unnecessarily lengthening the time it takes to bring a new hire into the company.

Some recruiters fail because they *under*manage the risk of hiring and training new salespeople. Too little concern for risk management can make some recruiters obsessed with image over substance. Others throw caution to the wind and become impulsive, impatient with details, and convinced that they are intuitive judges of character and talent (see question #6). These vain, self-glorifying individuals may look good and sound good and will often impress top management with their bravado and daring. But they can be toxic to most sales organizations. Inconsistent and unpredictable, dysfunctional managers devalue training and prefer to rely on non-skill-based competencies like charm and glibness. When recruiters undermanage risks, they can create distrust, reduce productivity, and increase turnover.

4. Lack of Training

Question #9 identifies still another cause of recruitment reluctance: a simple lack of training. A common theme we hear from struggling recruiters is their reliance on techniques picked up from a previous job or from the war stories of other recruiters that don't seem to match their current situation. The field of selling is undergoing tremendous changes, especially in response to the growth of the Internet and the explosion of high-tech sales organizations spawned by the information revolution. Out-of-touch veterans may not be getting the job done because they don't, won't, or can't understand and appreciate the changes brought about by the plugged-in generation. If you answered question #5 as true, you may be in this category and need to update your skill set as a recruiter.

The high-dollar, high-tech sale is completely different from the direct sales of a generation ago and is changing the paradigm of what makes a successful rep. Today the stereotype of the backslapping, jovial joke teller is as dead as the typewriter. Salespeople today are far more likely to be cerebral and technical in their approach. Sales cycles are longer and more complex than a generation ago because consumers have access to more information. It used to be that high-tech recruiters could work within their own industries and environments. Today, every industry is being impacted by the global economy. Salespeople have to know more and work faster and smarter than ever before. Young buyers demand information and are less likely to make purchases based on hype or out of any loyalty to a product. Products are available today through many more distribution channels than existed in years past. If a customer doesn't like the way the automobile salesperson pressured him into a sale, he can go online and buy the same car.

As a recruiter, you have to keep current with changes like these and how they can impact your search for top talent. The changing landscape of sales marketing requires that recruiters be better informed than ever before. That's the value of Hire Performance. Consider it your textbook for proven sales-recruiting technologies. Approach these chapters with an open, inquiring mind. Some subjects will be familiar and easy to grasp. Others may require more time.

CONCLUSION

Recruiting is perhaps the most difficult type of sale there is. For the same reason a river never rises higher than its source, managers and employers who are reluctant to recruit will struggle to put together a winning sales team. In this chapter we examined four causes of recruitment reluctance:

- contact hesitation—the emotional need to avoid the very people who can make a difference in what we earn
- poor sales identity—a negative view of salespeople and selling
- poor risk management—over- or undercompensating for the pressure of not making a hiring mistake
- lack of training—outdated information

Identify any areas of recruitment reluctance and address them—now!

4

STRATEGIC RECRUITING

You've probably seen that test that begins with the instruction "Read through all the questions on this test before attempting to answer the problems," followed by a long list of complicated questions. The kicker comes at the very end when the last item on the page instructs you to only complete the first problem and ignore the rest. Impatience can get the better of us every time. Perhaps you, too, see a problem and start solving it before assessing the whole situation. Patience is not always seen as a virtue in today's fast-paced business environment, but if you want to succeed, you must develop a strategy for success and not merely a collection of tactics.

Recruiting a winning sales team doesn't happen accidentally. It requires strategic thinking and planning. The word "strategic" describes a long-term, big-picture perspective. Strategic recruiting implies more than a few gimmicky how-tos. You need to know the who-tos and whys. Hire Performance is a recruiting strategy to help you avoid the three worst mistakes recruiters make.

THE THREE WORST MISTAKES RECRUITERS MAKE

RECRUITER MISTAKE #1—RUSHING TO RECRUIT

The worst mistake recruiters make is to ignore strategic planning and just barge ahead with the task, trusting in intuition and luck, improvising quick fixes to long-term problems. It's easy to do. Busy managers can certainly justify the rush. You don't have the time or resources to dedicate to deliberation.

It's hard to resist the pressure to hurry up and fill a position. Your top producer suddenly resigns. Your boss is pushing hard for more recruits. You're losing market share to your competitor. Situations like this add pressure to the already stress-filled assignment of recruiting talented sales professionals. But small mistakes at the beginning often have catastrophic consequences later on. In the same way that a rocket firing a fraction of a second late can cause it to miss its target in space by a large margin, a small mistake at the outset of your recruitment efforts can cost you thousands of dollars and hours of grief down range.

The best thing you can do as you begin the task of recruiting a winning sales team is to slow down. Think about what you're doing and how you want to go about doing it. Plan for course corrections, controls, and contingencies. If you discipline yourself to go a little slower at the beginning, you'll make fewer mistakes later. And the mistakes you do make will probably be less catastrophic. Strategic planning means less backtracking, which ultimately allows you to go faster.

The faster you go, the blurrier the view outside your window. Getting in a hurry to hire can also distort your perspective. You're not as thorough as you might be about checking into details. The temptation to take shortcuts increases. You may not want to take a hard look at negative information, particularly if you've already invested several interviews with a candidate. It's easy to rationalize a bad hire as the most cost-effective strategy, but soon you're back at square one, looking for a replacement. Only now you've got to regain what you lost in hiring the wrong person.

But time pressures aren't the only reason managers rush the hiring process. Many recruiters never clearly define the attributes, skills, experiences, and key competencies necessary to the position they are trying to fill. This leads to …

RECRUITER MISTAKE #2—CLONING

If you don't define a strategy, you will very likely end up making the second big mistake of recruiting: hiring people who are just like you.

For example, Janet was promoted to regional sales manager because of her success in the field. Her boss told her that the company expected her to clone herself.

"Find people like you," the VP of sales told her. "Find us five more 'Janets.'"

Janet believed that she could spot the right candidate intuitively, since after all she herself was the recruitment template. This is a huge mistake. Your kids, your significant other, or your dog can think you're the benchmark of greatness, but that won't cut it in business. Hiring personality clones inserts an invisible bias into your selection process. When you use yourself as a model, ego gets in the way and undermines your ability to objectively evaluate the right person for the job. Some call hiring people like themselves "the mirroring effect." It's a prescription for productivity problems and high turnover.

Organizations thrive when different social styles and personality types interact. Salespeople and their managers have preferred ways of getting things done. These preferences, when taken together, form styles. Salespeople develop a selling style. Recruiters develop a recruiting style based on their preferences and habits. Diversity of styles on a team promotes creativity and productivity. Strengths in one individual help compensate for another's deficiencies. When people cooperate and complement each other's efforts, teamwork galvanizes and improves the bottom line as well. The more styles you build into your sales team, the more likely you are to intersect a broader cross-section of customer styles and needs and consequently sell more. Homogeneity is good for milk, bad for sales organizations. When managers attempt to clone themselves, they undermine team synergy.

Do you know your behavioral style? How do you instinctively react to problems and opportunities? How do you prefer to communicate?

Are you naturally more task oriented or relationship oriented? How do you like to be treated by salespeople when you buy something? These and many more details of daily life define your behavioral style (which we'll discuss in chapter 8). Until you understand your own preferences and sales predispositions, you don't really know if you can or should trust your gut instincts when hiring salespeople. Blindly following your instincts could be catastrophic to your recruitment efforts. You need objective feedback. That's why the first person who needs to be evaluated in the strategic process of recruiting a winning sales team is you, the recruiter.

I strongly recommend that you complete our SalesKey assessment or some other validated profile of behavior selling style as soon as possible. If you take your time and don't try to manipulate or second-guess your responses, you will gain valuable insights into your style. If you don't want to take an assessment, you should talk with another recruiter who knows you well and ask for objective feedback on how you come across. If you are on good terms with your supervisor, you might get valuable insights about your style from that source as well. You'll know what to look for after reading the rest of this book, but you need to know your own communication strengths and challenges.

Over and over we see this mistake repeat itself, unfortunately often with the same managers. A few years back Robinson had a manager, let's call her Becky, call to review a candidate's SalesKey. She wanted to hire a candidate whose profile indicated problems with prospecting behaviors. "You don't understand, Matt," Becky enthused. "This guy is fantastic. He's exactly like I was when I was a rep." This was partially true, as they both had similar personality types.

"I am glad you like his personality, because the objective evidence suggests he is not going to pick up the phone," said Robinson. Becky ignored this and hired the individual because she liked him. The recruiter ignored the objective suggestion that her candidate did not like prospecting. It might sound a bit absurd, but the newly hired personality clone lasted exactly three days, resigning because he didn't realize he would have to generate all his own leads. To make matters worse, when Becky hired the failed rep's replacement, round two began.

"I know you're going to tell me, 'I told you so,' but I have this new candidate I am talking to. She is fantastic. Comes from a very well-respected employer and just wants to be closer to home."

Robinson said he understood her enthusiasm, but the objective data contained in her SalesKey profile was clear—the second candidate would also not like the prospecting aspect of the job. Becky ignored the evidence a second time, insisting that her second recruit was different; she was sure of it. Perfect personality and all (by the way, another carbon copy of the manager), Becky was going with her gut reaction. The second outcome was worse, lasting only until lunchtime her first day on the job and never heard from again.

RECRUITER MISTAKE #3—IGNORING THE COST OF FAILURE

Without a recruitment strategy, managers are blind to the true costs of a bad hire. We call this shortsighted condition *flop myopia*. Do you know what a hiring mistake costs? It may be a lot more than you think. Here's a series of steps to take to help you calculate the true cost of failure.

1. First, add up all the hard costs of your hiring process. Here are just a few examples of items in that list:
    - price of running ads on the Internet or in the local paper
    - cost of printing brochures, fliers, and other recruitment pieces (don't forget the cost of developing these items as well)
    - running credit checks or Department of Motor Vehicle reports (this step can save recruiters a lot of grief later on)
    - expenses for travel, meals, or renting off-site interview facilities when necessary
    - value of your time in preparation as well as the actual interview process (Too many entrepreneurs undervalue their time. It's a precious commodity you lose and can never recover when you hire a poor performer.)
    - contractor or employee setup costs (legal costs to draw up the contract, entering worker information into

the payroll system or updating computer programs, complying with local, state, federal regulations, etc.)

2. Second, add in your training costs. Most companies spend more today on training than ever before. The days are long gone when all the sales recruiter needed was a yarn of "unlimited opportunity," a presentation book, some order forms, and a hearty "go get 'em, Tiger." The marketplace has changed. Selling involves more technical specialties than ever. Here are some common training costs:
   - cost of training materials (workshops or materials you purchase or the cost of developing them yourself)
   - cost of samples
   - computers, presentation books, and other sales aids
   - expenses for travel, meals, or renting training facilities
   - value of the trainer's time

3. Finally, add in your lost-opportunity costs. Making a bad hire deprives your firm of income you might have realized if you had recruited a top performer. Here's the formula to figure lost-opportunity costs:
   - Calculate the income of your top producer, or better yet, your competitor's top producer.
   - Subtract the average income generated by your previous bad hires.
   - Multiply that figure by the number of bad hires.
   - Depending on your business, you may also have to calculate into your lost-opportunity costs the value of lost customers and reduced goodwill. Word gets around. You know that competitors are having trouble. If you get a reputation for high turnover or low morale, you compound lost-opportunity costs by making it even more difficult to attract top-quality candidates.

Knowing the real value of a bad hire can provide you with a benchmark against which to evaluate the effectiveness of any tool or tactic you incorporate into your recruitment strategy. For example, what is the cost of an assessment or a background check as compared to the cost of a bad hire? Is it a reasonable investment?

Strategic recruiting helps avoid many of these costly errors. The boss may only be concerned about filling a certain number of employment slots every month, but professional recruiters know that it takes more to produce a winning sales team. Recruiting must be personally satisfying as well as profitable. Recruiters need to define for themselves, if no one else, why their work is important and whom it helps. Money alone is not enough of a motivating force to sustain the top-gun recruiter. The reason so many recruiters become burned out, cynical, discouraged, and disillusioned is because they have not developed a personal recruiting strategy that incorporates personal values into their daily work product. Cut off from spiritual purpose, work becomes drudgery.

YOUR RECRUITING STRATEGY STATEMENT

One way we recommend thinking more strategically about your recruiting is to write your your own recruitment strategy statement. This is a declaration of how you want to recruit and why. It's your philosophy of recruiting—the fusion of values, beliefs, and assumptions that emerge from your unique experiences. It summarizes what you do, how you want to accomplish your goal, and perhaps the purpose for getting up and facing another day of calling, interviewing, and selling your opportunity. Your recruiting strategy statement should help you do a better job of recruiting by clarifying and focusing your energy.

Your strategy statement provides guidelines and benchmarks for dealing with your clients, customers, and suppliers. It guides your thinking and acting in ambiguous situations and reduces ambiguity and tension if conflict erupts. For example, if providing exceptional service really is your mission, you might be less inclined to argue with others who share the selection decision than to approach disagreements in a spirit of collaborative problem solving. Keeping your core values and goals front and center prevents short-term situations from derailing your long-term aspirations.

Your recruiting strategy statement can reveal inconsistent or conflicting attitudes that could negatively impact recruiting. For example, you may be driven to succeed in your career, but you may also carry around inside you a need to be liked and accepted by nearly everyone you meet. These incompatible forces pull you in opposite directions. So, if you do nothing as a way of avoiding potential conflict, it's quite probable that your recruiting will suffer because you can't comfortably say no to people you want to like you.

Your recruiting strategy statement maximizes your strengths and minimizes your weaknesses. If you value carefulness and believe that it's important to avoid taking unnecessary risks, your approach to hiring will look very different from someone who relies more heavily on intuition and the power of first impressions. Without examining your assumptions about people and work, your recruiting style might fit you as badly as a size 10 shoe on a size 13 foot.

Your recruiting strategy statement can help provide stability in uncertain times. The unexpected always happens. Good people quit. Products change. Your competitor lowers prices. Personnel changes and market shifts aren't nearly as likely to knock you off balance if you've identified your philosophy and keep the bigger picture constantly in front of you. Your recruitment philosophy can keep you focused on what is really important and help guide your responses as you identify what is productive and what is wasteful; what is important and what is merely interesting; what is urgent and what is necessary; what moves you closer to your target; and what is ultimately distracting and destructive of your goals.

THE HIRE PERFORMANCE PHILOSOPHY OF RECRUITING

We want to be up front with you about our assumptions about recruiting. You don't have to agree with our viewpoint entirely to use the Hire Performance system effectively. But it's only fair that we share with you some of our basic beliefs and values before asking you to identify yours.

> Selling is first and always a people business. People come
> first. People can make doing business lousy or great.

> Recruiting and hiring are human activities that can never be replaced with machines or tests, because the most important thing about an individual (character, work ethic, integrity, motivation) can only be discerned by another human being who possesses these same attributes.
>
> Therefore, our strategy requires that we maintain good character, integrity, a strong work ethic, and motivation so that we will discern excellence and select candidates on the basis of personal qualifications first and professional experience and skills second. Skills can be taught; character cannot. Experience comes easily. Integrity is the hard part.

It's probably a little too wordy for needlepoint. We have yet to discover the one-size-fits-all recruiting strategy statement. We are strongly service-motivated—putting people ahead of just about everything else. That's not necessarily "right" or admirable or even profitable. But it is what we believe and will definitely influence our recommendations for your recruiting.

Your viewpoint could be completely different. It probably is. Some recruiters can say, "I come first. I'm interested in getting results for me." Still another manager might candidly admit, "I want something simple, uncomplicated, and reliable that will make me look good to my boss." Fine. Whatever it is, put it out there. Take a look at it. Evaluate it. Does it work to sustain you in tough times? Is it powerful enough to motivate you to get out of your comfort zone?

Although we're focusing on behaviors in this book, that doesn't mean that we're only looking at surface issues. Those behaviors are reliable clues to character. Many recruiters and managers today make the mistake of hiring for skills and then training for work values and team values. But it's always easier and far less expensive to hire people who are honest, hard-working, and socially outgoing and then teach them how to sell your product than it is to teach people experienced in your business how to smile, how to get along with people, and that it's wrong to steal.

CONCLUSION

In this chapter we identified three short-sighted mistakes recruiters often make. They are

1. rushing to recruit in response to various pressures;
2. cloning—making ourselves the hiring template; and
3. ignoring the cost of failure, which can and should motivate recruiters to view their task more strategically.

We identified our own recruiting strategy statement in hopes that, if you haven't already done so, you will define your own recruiting philosophy containing what you believe about people and recruiting as well as lay out why what you do is important to you and those who pay for your service. Yes, it may slow you down a little now to organize your thoughts and define your strategy. But in the long run, you'll go faster and ultimately get the jump on your competition.

5

THE FOUR LEVELS OF SALES

Selling is developmental. In the same way a baby learns to crawl before attempting to walk or run, higher levels of sales productivity depend on mastering lower-level skills, aptitudes, and challenges. One of the great failings of most sales recruiters is not knowing what comes first, second, and third in the development of a salesperson. Without these priorities, you won't know what to look for in prospective salespeople. Here's an example of what we mean. One sales bestseller that claims to be "research-based" says the best predictor of top sales talent is ... (drum roll please) ... the ability to ask good questions. Of course, probing has always been an important sales skill. But if you think about it a moment, the ability to ask good questions doesn't come first; it presumes another activity. What has to come before a rep can ask great questions? The salesperson has to get in front of a prospect. Developmentally, what difference does it make if someone can ask great questions if he or she doesn't talk to enough people? Recruiters need to make sure that a prospective employee has no contact hesitation before being concerned about communication skills.

To clarify the process of developing productive salespeople, Dr. Barnett created a sales developmental model called *the Four Levels of Sales* (see figure 1).

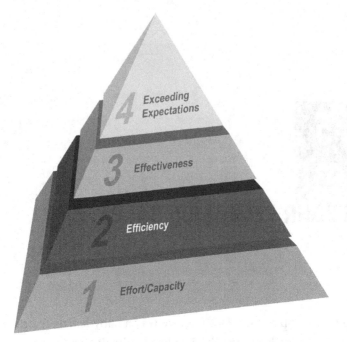

Figure 1: The Four Levels of Sales

We portray the Four Levels in the shape of a triangle because sales development is a hierarchy; that is, each successive level depends on the successful completion of the previous stage. Like Abraham Maslow's famous hierarchy of needs, when a basic need (such as safety) is satisfied, then one may begin working on higher level drives.

This model can apply to any job. But we are concerned here with how salespeople develop. Each level is made up of a cluster of behaviors that are integral to attaining certain benchmarks of sales productivity. To help make them easier to remember, we identify each level with a word that starts with the letter E.

LEVEL 1: EFFORT AND CAPACITY

We identify Level 1 sales development with the words effort and capacity. Effort describes how hard someone is willing to work. Capacity looks at the basic aptitudes a person must have to function in a sales role. Both of these are equally important. Some people have terrific skills and experience to perform at peak levels of performance in a sales career. However, they don't want to work hard, so their capacity is held hostage to poor effort. On the other hand, an individual may be a hard worker, put in long hours, and still not develop into a productive salesperson. In this case, their effort cannot overcome certain deficiencies in capacity that every sales job demands.

Hire Performance means making Level 1 behaviors the starting point for evaluating any sales candidate. These attributes are foundational. The applicant must bring these behaviors with him or her to the new sales job, because Level 1 behaviors are not cost-effective to train. We're not saying that Level 1 behaviors will always be the most important behaviors to predict productivity, but they do come first in the recruitment process. If Level 1 is deficient, there's nothing upon which to build the rest of a salesperson's development. We will identify the specific behaviors that make up Level 1 in the next chapter.

LEVEL 2: EFFICIENCY

Level 2 behaviors are about the efficiency of the salesperson. By efficiency we mean can the individual learn the company's products and internal systems to get the information he or she needs to work quickly without a lot of mistakes. Level 2 behaviors focus on cognitive skills. What kind of learner is the individual? Will it cost more to train a candidate because he or she can't focus on critical tasks at hand? Level 2 does not replace Level 1 but builds upon it. Think about what happens immediately after someone is hired. Usually the new hire is expected to successfully complete a training program that introduces company resources and product knowledge. Level 2 behaviors are those that enable the rep to solve customer problems and meet prospects' needs efficiently.

LEVEL 3: EFFECTIVENESS

Level 3 looks at the effectiveness of the salesperson in communicating with all kinds of customers and prospects. Four communication styles are identified in Level 3. A style is a collection of predictable behaviors that satisfy an emotional need. Again, think of the typical onboarding of a new employee. After training the new hire in systems and products, the salesperson is likely given sales training on how to most effectively communicate with prospects and customers about these specific products and services.

LEVEL 4: EXCEEDING EXPECTATIONS

Finally, we reach the pinnacle of the sales-development hierarchy. At Level 4 the focus is on exceeding expectations. Top producers who have attained Levels 1, 2, and 3 reach a point where they are seeing so many customers that they simply can't work any harder, so they have to work smarter and develop new avenues of business development. For example, can the salesperson comfortably talk with groups of prospects instead of one buyer at a time? Can the top-performing rep increase the size of his or her average sale and thus increase productivity? Few salespeople attain Level 4, but those who do can usually generate more productivity by leveraging one Level 4 behavior than the company would realize from hiring lots of new reps.

Using the Four Levels of Sales Pyramid, it's easy to see why the sales-training program that made asking questions the secret to selling simply can't deliver on its promise of sales success. We're not saying that probing skills aren't important. But interacting with customers is a higher-order behavior that belongs at Level 3. The ability to ask questions is only going to pay off with salespeople who are already performing competently at Levels 1 (putting in the effort) and 2 (knowing how to efficiently navigate the company's systems).

THE POWER OF THE PYRAMID

The Four Levels of Sales Pyramid helps the recruiter do three things that directly impact the ability to excel in the search for sales talent.

1. Recognize Recruiting Priorities

The Four Levels of Sales Pyramid helps recruiters recognize the skills that must have priority in the job search. We've seen the checklist of skills and experience recruiters are asked to recruit to. Only the ability to walk on water is omitted. Often it's a grab bag of clichés ("able to work in a fast-paced environment") and subjective qualities ("drive," "determination to succeed"). When we ask why those attributes were chosen, hands fly up and outward in a who-knows gesture. This is why we start each new client engagement with a study of the current sales force. We hate to say this, but the truth is that most businesses have no idea what makes someone a good or mediocre salesperson. We know this because so few sales organizations track behavioral metrics, only sales results. Because many hiring authorities see selling as an art rather than a science, they are prone to the most inefficient of recruiting strategies—throw enough stuff against the wall and hope something sticks. Anyone with that approach doesn't know the behavioral priorities and is going to waste time and resources playing odds stacked against the recruiter.

The Four Levels of Sales Pyramid provides you with a template to help you know what comes first, second, and third in the development of a competent salesperson, helping you recognize your recruiting priorities.

2. Diagnose Relative Strengths and Deficiencies

The Four Levels of Sales Pyramid helps the recruiter diagnose and leverage relative strengths and deficiencies in a candidate. For example, if Level 1 behaviors aren't in place, you don't have a firm foundation on which to build. That person just isn't going to develop into a productive salesperson. Any applicant weak in Level 1 should never be considered at all for a sales position. However, if Level 1 is strong but there are deficiencies at Level 2 or Level 3, there could still be a chance that a candidate could succeed in the right organization. The Four Levels of Sales Pyramid allows you to gauge the relative importance of a candidate's strengths and challenges. It tells you what you can safely ignore and what you dare not take for granted.

3. Predict Specific Training Issues

Within each of the levels of the Four Levels of Sales Pyramid are specific behaviors. If a rep is deficient in Level 2, the recruiter can specifically pinpoint the type of training that will be needed. Knowing specifically where the applicant is going to need special attention helps the recruiter to make informed recommendations to hiring authorities. For example, someone with deficient computer skills (a Level 2 behavior) may be able to function quite well selling cars but will require remedial training for employment in a high-tech call center. Or the person who prefers to work alone rather than depend on a team may do just fine managing a territory but could have serious productivity issues in a sales office setting. The recruiter can improve his or her success ratio by knowing the targeted training needs of a candidate.

Without a systematic way of understanding what makes salespeople successful, the recruiter can be at best only reactive rather than proactive. Not knowing the sequence and substance of specific skills makes recruiting inefficient and ineffective. The Four Levels of Sales Pyramid rescues recruiting from hit-or-miss tactics and allows the recruiter to work a proven strategy to build a winning sales team.

DIFFERENT TYPES OF SELLING

We know that every sales organization is unique. The Four Levels apply regardless of the type of selling carried on. Here are the three major types of sales.

1. Direct Sales

This type of selling is usually person-to-person. It can be done face-to-face or over the phone. The sales rep is usually responsible for finding prospects and filling a pipeline of potential buyers who are at various stages in the sales process. Typically in direct sales, almost everyone is a prospect for what you sell. Because of the need to prospect in most direct sales, Level 1 effort and capacity behaviors are absolutely critical. Can the salesperson pick up the phone and dial a sufficient number of times each day to achieve production goals? Or if expected to leave his or her place of employment, will the rep put in the effort of a long day initiating contacts with current and prospective buyers? Examples of direct sales include manufacturer's reps, pharmaceutical sales, brokerage houses, and food service.

2. Strategic Sales

Strategic selling is typically team-to-team; that is, there are multiple decision makers for the client while on the sales side, strategic salespeople may work with a team of engineers, accountants, and design people. Strategic selling involves long sales cycles and very costly expenditures (hundreds of thousands of dollars or more). One of our clients manufactures MRI machines that cost about a million dollars each. It can take months, sometimes even a year or more, to work through the complexity of such a big-ticket sale. In strategic sales, prospecting is usually not as important as in direct sales, because most if not all potential buyers in a given territory are already identified. For example, the MRI manufacturer knows all the medical users in a territory. But strategic selling still requires effort and a capacity for teamwork. The strategic salesperson must stay in regular contact with decision makers, keep up a steady flow of communication about next steps in the sales process, monitor deadlines, and keep everyone on the team informed. Examples of strategic sales include almost any high-end technology (phone systems, servers, etc.), institutional brokerage sales, franchise selling, and consultant sales.

3. Inbound Sales

This type of selling occurs when marketing campaigns drive prospects to a toll-free number or a local meeting for more information. It can also reflect the typical retail sales environment. Inbound salespeople are often trained to close sales in one call. The process can be very transactional because the sales rep is completely reactionary; he or she doesn't initiate the contact at all. The effort and capacity of inbound sales has to do with a person's tolerance for repetitive activity. More and more, retailers are encouraging salespeople to follow up with prospects who didn't buy the first time. Many customer-service people are being trained to add value to the company by making recommendations and then referring current customers to a sales rep. Cross-selling and up-selling are forms of inbound sales. Examples include car sales, department store sales, and almost any customer-service call center.

The Four Levels Pyramid can be applied to all these variants of the profession. Although each type of sales environment may demand slight alterations in the underlying behaviors used in each level, the four Es are consistent as a model for approaching the task of sales recruiting.

CONCLUSION

This chapter introduces the recruiter to the Four Levels of Sales Pyramid, a hierarchy of prioritized behaviors common to all productive salespeople.

- Level 1 focuses on the salesperson's effort and capacity to perform the essential tasks of the position.
- Level 2 focuses on the cognitive and teamwork skills that make people efficient in their selling.
- Level 3 focuses on effective communication with customers.
- Level 4 focuses on ways for good reps to exceed expectations to become even more productive.

Regardless of the type of selling (direct, strategic, or inbound), knowing the Four Levels helps the proactive recruiter recognize recruiting priorities, diagnose the relative importance of strengths and deficiencies, and predict specific training needs.

6

SIX BEHAVIORS OF LEVEL 1

In the last chapter, we said that Level 1 consists of behaviors that impact how hard a person is likely to work (effort) and helps predict the individual's potential to perform the essential tasks of a sales job (capacity). This applies to any kind of sales job, whether it's direct sales, strategic sales, or inbound sales. But what specific behaviors are we looking for?

Here are the all-important six behaviors that determine an individual's Level 1 effort and capacity and provide the foundation for all further sales development.

1. ENERGY

Energy is the can-do of Level 1. It's stamina; it's health; it's the key component of effort. Without sufficient energy, salespeople make fewer contacts, which in turn leads to fewer sales. Reps run out of steam and are ready to rest during prime selling time. Low-energy individuals are prone to making fewer contacts because they don't work as hard or as long as someone with good energy management.

Top producers consistently bring higher levels of energy to their career than do poor producers. In cross-industry studies, we found that upper-echelon salespeople average 30 percent more energy than mediocre performers. High-energy individuals are more likely to have regular exercise programs, get an adequate amount of sleep, refrain from drug use (including alcohol and tobacco), and maintain an appropriate body weight. With more energy, salespeople are also more likely to manage stress better than tired, overweight salespeople.

Outside direct sales typically require more energy than inside sales. Too much energy can cause a phone rep to become restless. We can quickly spot the high-energy salespeople when we visit call centers. They are the people pacing back and forth like lions in a cage, burning excess energy as they talk to customers. Generally, good energy means that people are able to work hard. They put in the effort.

A warning: Just because someone is enthusiastic and talks a mile a minute in a job interview does not necessarily mean that he or she has the kind of physical stamina required for sales. Some people perform as energetic go-getters in an interview, but it may be an act to get the job. Once hired, the effervescent personality may merely distract and can easily create productivity problems. Energy is not about how excited people can get in a job interview but how many contacts they can make.

Organizations have a huge impact on the amount of energy sales reps bring to their daily tasks. Too many sales meetings create a sedentary, less-energetic sales team. Unrealistic performance quotas can also erode energy. One of the biggest energy drains in organizations is restructuring and downsizing. Reorganization drains energy by increasing stress levels and directing energy away from the primary task of selling to coping with change.

So, besides looking at the energy scale of SalesKey, how can you assess an individual's energy? Here are two things you can do.

1. Look at the individual's pace of movement and speaking. You don't need a sophisticated assessment to evaluate energy. Use your eyes and ears. People have a speed at which they walk and talk. Assuming the individual does not have a disability, does your candidate move slowly or is she quick and lithe to stand and move? Does he speak without needing to stop and take a breath?

In our experience one company that gets this right is Apple. They recruit energetic people. One of us (Barnett) recently went to the local Apple store, where the greeter called Jessica over to provide help. Jessica's countenance lit up as she moved quickly to help. Her handshake was firm but not overpowering. Her voice was articulate and projected vigor. Now, before you reach the conclusion that this was some kid, you should know that Jessica is a mother of five! Okay, so now you know how she stays so energetic. But from the moment she came alongside the customer, she projected a lively get-up-and-go that made the sales conversation invigorating.

2. Ask about hobbies. Hobbies are a clue to a person's energy levels. The person whose leisure pursuit is going to movies, reading, or stamp collecting is likely to be less energetic than someone who spends free time playing sports, jogging, or hiking. Many sales organizations that recruit on college campuses look specifically for athletes. Henry Schein Dental has found this to be a winning strategy. "We've had great success recruiting student athletes right out of college," says Dean Kyle, head of the southwest sales region. "They are competitive and bring lots of energy to what they do, and they work well on teams." If you're looking for entry-level salespeople, we think Dean is on to something.

We will share some specific interview questions with you in a later chapter to help you identify how much energy a person brings to the job.

2. GOAL MOTIVATION

Goal motivation is the want-to of sales. Great salespeople are almost always strongly motivated to achieve the goals they set for themselves. Companies can set sales quotas and lots of other productivity goals. But unless an individual is intrinsically motivated to achieve his or her own version of excellence, corporate goals will go unheeded. In study after study, we see strong correlations with the SalesKey goal scale and above-average sales production. The strength of a person's goals has a lot to say about the effort and capacity of a salesperson to achieve success.

We still think one of the best questions to use to lead off an interview is the old standby: "Tell me where you want to be in five years. What are your personal goals?" This is a great lead-off question because:

- The candidate expects it and is probably prepared to answer it.
- It lets the applicant begin talking and breaking the ice.

Don't blow off the answer or get distracted by the details of what the applicant says. Listen for goal specificity and the motivating power of that goal. You should hear energy behind this goal. Watch his or her face as she talks about her ambitions. Does she smile? Does he light up talking about the outcome he anticipates? If the candidate doesn't react emotionally when telling you about a goal, it's phony baloney, a piece of theater meant to make an impression. It's not truly motivating. Great reps will always have something greater than themselves to keep them going in tough times, a goal that transcends winning awards, keeping one's job, or even making money. Intrinsic goals almost always involve people important to the rep, and not merely buying things. Extrinsic goals are more frequently self-centered and self-protective.

Many top performers got that way because they connected their daily work to a deeply meaningful, personal goal. Goal-driven reps are much more likely than mediocre reps to break down personal goals and sales targets into manageable daily activities. Almost intuitively, salespeople with strong goal motivation know how many contacts, how many conversations, and how many times they need to ask for the business each day if they are going to succeed. Poor-performing salespeople are less likely to know their activity ratios. Or, even if they know them, they do not manage their work by these objective statistics. Struggling salespeople prefer more subjective, feeling-oriented evaluations of performance.

As an example, consider Sara. She never did well on tests in school. Even though she knew the material, Sara had a bad habit of tensing up when she had to answer questions. Today Sara is a salesperson who gets quite uptight just thinking about her new quota of fifty phone calls a day.

She gets bored easily and finds it difficult to screen out distractions when phone time rolls around. In fact, Sara seems to invite interruptions, welcoming coworkers into her cubicle to chat about the latest movie or to discuss a recent call with a difficult customer.

Sara is struggling with the Level 1 issue of getting goal motivated. There could be many reasons for her behavior—performance anxiety or attention deficit disorder, just to name a couple. But the reasons for the behavior really aren't important; it's the outcome we're concerned about. Even if we knew the origins of Sara's goal aversion, it would be extremely cost-prohibitive to try to change it (unless Sara is a top producer, and then it *may* be worth the investment). But it's unlikely that Sara or any salesperson who resists setting goals is going to rise to the top. When her manager asked about Sara's failure to reach her fifty-call quota, she said that it's more important for employees to feel appreciated and respected than to reduce their efforts to a numbers game.

Sometimes the problem is personal, as in Sara's case. But many times organizations undermine goal motivation in their employees by intentionally or unintentionally refusing to provide objective activity-based sales ratios to their new hires. Firms that only measure sales results sometimes substitute subjective performance measures (number of mistakes on applications, following a prescribed sales script, etc.). Whether the firm celebrates efficiency or customer-satisfaction scores or policy compliance, taking the focus off sales and putting it onto these ancillary goals creates and sustains emotional barriers in the rep to goal motivation. It communicates to employees that their personal goals are not important to the company. The only things that count are what the company wants. This promotes higher turnover and lowers employee morale.

Good salespeople set goals; highly productive salespeople are energized by their sales targets on a daily basis. Sales slackers are distracted by the search for shortcuts to get around quotas or to justify keeping busy with nonselling activities.

Here are two ways to evaluate a candidate's goal motivation.

1. Ask the person with sales experience about his or her contact activity in the previous sales position. If the candidate can tell

you his or her exact sales metrics without complaining about the numbers, that applicant is probably sufficiently goal motivated. Another question you can ask during the hiring interview is about the kind of manager the candidate prefers to work with. Does she expect the manager to keep her motivated? Does he want a manager who is hands off, "someone who won't smother me" or "micromanage"? Drill down on this answer. Find out why the candidate dislikes micromanaging. Is the problem that he or she doesn't really want to be held accountable? Does the applicant take responsibility for encouraging her own top performance, or does he expect others to supply the motivation?

2. Look at income history. Be careful about hiring someone who has an income history that is significantly less than will be required in the role they are moving into. If your organization needs a rep to be making $150,000 a year and for the last three years your candidate has earned $90,000 tops, that individual may have adjusted his or her expectations to lower earnings. Someone who is willing to work on the cheap is not necessarily a good find. The goal motivation may not be there to do enough to increase his or her paycheck by $60,000 per year. It's critical to get on the same page about income expectations. Learn to ask, "Why would the extra income be important to you? What would you do with the extra $60,000?" Sometimes we make HR a little nervous with this question, but we are not doing someone a favor by setting them up to fail because they have lowered their personal expectations to less than what may be needed in the new job. The more specific an individual's goals, the more likely you are to see stronger effort and capacity.

3. SALES IDENTITY

Sales identity is essential for identifying a potential salesperson's capacity to succeed. Jack is an example of how a poor sales identity destroys careers.

Jack decided to accept a sales job after an injury cut short his career in baseball. A friend invited him into his home improvement business. He was paid to find prospects in a community by going door to door. This began to get under Jack's skin. He began to feel the work was demeaning. He grew more and more bitter and felt he deserved better, but he was desperate and had no other job prospects at the time that paid as well. He hated door-to-door cold calling and searched for ways of psyching himself up to go into neighborhoods and make calls. Jack did what a lot of reps with a sales-identity crisis do. He got addicted to motivational programs. From his days in sports, Jack knew how important it was to have the right mental attitude before going into the big game. So, Jack spent more and more time and money on self-help books and CDs for the car. He didn't know it at the time, but Jack was probably making his case of poor sales identity even worse. Rather than knocking on doors, Jack spent the afternoon in his car reading or listening to motivational gurus. It took longer and longer for him to psych himself up. One day Jack burst into his manager's office, threw his presentation book on the desk, and quit.

Sales identity is the degree to which the individual values a sales career. It's very difficult to consciously or subconsciously hate selling and succeed in sales. Sales identity is a critical Level 1 behavior that any candidate for a sales job must bring to the position. The company cannot and should not have to train its people to want to sell.

There are three ways you can use to evaluate someone's sales identity without looking at the SalesKey sales-identity score.

1. Ask your applicant about what he or she thinks is society's view of salespeople today. Individuals with poor sales identity will often uncritically accept negative stereotypes of salespeople. This is especially true with jobs that involve selling on the telephone. Opt-out lists and other regulatory impediments to telemarketers have made it difficult for people in phone sales to even tell others what they do.

2. If your applicant has sales experience, inquire about the job title given to sales in his previous employment. If the person is new to sales, check his résumé for how he describes the position

he hopes to get. Chances are good that if that job title is some euphemism for sales, the candidate may have a serious Level 1 issue for which your training cannot compensate. Companies help create a poor sales identity by creating euphemisms for their salespeople. Instead of advertising for "salespeople," employment ads are for "account managers," "advisors," or "consultants." Not only does renaming the sales function tend to attract individuals who have already been infected with a poor sales identity, like Jack, but it also corrupts people like Melissa who wanted to get into sales. She thought she was responding to an ad for entry-level salespeople. She got the job. But on her first day of training, her manager said, "Look, we don't call ourselves 'salespeople' here." "I didn't know what to think," Melissa said. "Are they going to ask me to do something unethical? What's wrong with selling that we have to be ashamed of what we do?"

3. Determine whether your candidate has ever turned down an offer to become a sales manager or take another position. Top sales reps love selling and probably wouldn't do anything else. Frequently strong sales-identity salespeople turn down the "promotion" to manager while employees with a less well-formed sales identity jump at the chance. Reps who don't, won't, or can't take responsibility for their career choice to be in sales are highly unlikely to break out of the ranks of mediocrity.

4. BALANCED RISK SENSITIVITY

Risk sensitivity helps predict the capacity of your applicant for dealing with the uncertainty that comes with every sales job. This behavior has three categories:

-   **High risk sensitivity** means the individual shies away from anything perceived to be uncertain or that could become a problem. This is one attribute most sales-personality tests usually get at least half right. People who don't like to take risks and worry too much don't usually do well in sales (unless it's a highly regulated industry or a job selling security in some form or another). High risk sensitivity tends to limit the capacity of a salesperson by making him or her less comfortable in unpredictable social settings. High risk sensitivity is driven by a strong need for stability. People who avoid risks enjoy lots of structure and typically don't work well under pressure. But few of the most introverted, doom-saying types ever apply for sales jobs in the first place. They know they aren't good at sales and self-select out of the process. However, people with high risk sensitivity make great troubleshooters and analysts and gravitate to procedural jobs, not people jobs.

- **Low risk sensitivity** means that the person enjoys living a little dangerously from time to time. It's like their need for stability is underdeveloped. They aren't afraid of taking risks. In fact, many times they aren't even aware of the risks involved in a situation. Their capacity for change is very high. They need the adrenaline rush of taking chances. In our research with terminated employees, we're not surprised to find lower-than-average risk-sensitivity scores for people fired for cause (they embezzled money or broke the rules).

You can't always spot low risk sensitivity. We remember Jody, a participant in one of our workshops. She had an extremely low risk-sensitivity score on her SalesKey profile. Before we met her we pictured a very unconventional individual, maybe with lots of tats and body piercings. Were we ever surprised when Jody turned out to be a sweet, rather conservatively dressed young lady. During the workshop she was quiet and didn't do any of the things usually associated with low-risk-sensitivity individuals (come back late from breaks, ask questions for effect, etc.). After the class was over, she wanted to speak with us about her results. We expressed our surprise at the low risk sensitivity. When we asked if she enjoyed taking risks, she said, "Yeah, that risk-sensitivity finding is absolutely true. I do motocross on the weekends. Very dangerous stuff. I love it."

It's important to keep risk takers focused on the daily behaviors that drive future success instead of sitting back and relaxing during a blockbuster quarter. With a great month or quarter underway, they may be oblivious to the potential for problems and slow up the prospecting; then the pipeline dries up and a down month or quarter inevitably follows.

- **Balanced risk sensitivity** means that the person's need for stability isn't so strong that it paralyzes initiative or overanalyzes the possibility of failure; neither is it too weak so as to blind the individual to the consequences of poor choices. A balanced risk sensitivity will make people both prudent and capable of getting a thrill from their work. Sometimes high-performing salespeople enjoy taking some moderate risk to reap the high reward of sales. At other times a heightened risk sensitivity can help motivate a salesperson who is getting behind on attaining their goals.

Here are three ways to determine an individual's risk sensitivity without using SalesKey:

1. Pay attention to the kind of leisure activities your candidate enjoys. The more risky the hobby, the more likely the individual could have problems working in a highly regulated environment or selling products or services that require sensitivity to risk.

2. Listen for risk-sensitivity keywords like "I worry that ..." or "I'm afraid I'll ..." These subconscious verbal triggers can indicate someone who will spend more time worrying than selling.

3. Be alert to security themes in your interview. Security themes include lots of questions about benefits, guarantees for customers, and job security.

Whether a candidate is high or low on their need for stability, the managerial response is the same. Keep the salesperson focused on the daily controllable activities that drive future results.

5. INITIATIVE

Initiative is the most important of the six behaviors of Level 1 sales development. There are many people who probably *can* sell, but the real differentiator between success and failure is whether they *will* sell. These are not the same thing. An individual may have all the attributes that enable them to work hard and desire to achieve their personal best, but without initiative, that energy will be frittered away in nonproductive ways. Initiative goes right to the heart of effort and capacity in Level 1.

Initiative describes the predisposition of a person to either approach or to avoid responsibility. Behavior is essentially binary; it's on or off. It's moving toward something or avoiding something. Every situation calls into analysis the degree to which you approach or avoid. Yes, you can also do nothing, but that's an avoidance tactic too. When it comes to uncovering business opportunities, salespeople must absolutely possess initiative. You are looking for people who do not hesitate to approach opportunity rather than to hang back due to some inconvenience or second-guessing potential trouble. People with initiative respond at every appropriate opportunity (and if risk sensitivity is low, sometimes every not-so-appropriate opportunity) to strike up a conversation with strangers. When salespeople show weak initiative, they make more excuses than contacts.

Initiative is a bigger problem for veteran salespeople, although some rookies may bring to their new career some unexamined bias against certain kinds of customers and contacts. A pharmaceutical rep may not even be aware of a discomfort contacting doctors, feeling intimidated by people perceived to be socially or intellectually superior. Still other salespeople hear horror stories of friends and family members burned in multilevel marketing schemes and decide to put their personal sphere of influence off limits to prospecting. Novices usually respond well to training that identifies initiative problems and gets avoidance reactions out of the rep's personal blind spot and into the open where they can be demystified. Learning a few basic skills is usually enough to overcome the neophyte's hesitation to prospect. But long-time sales veterans who have sold to a specific clientele using a specific method for many years learn to cherry-pick the best accounts. They stop prospecting like they used to when they were building their business, relying instead on a highly developed network of referrals. Managers may even encourage this behavior. Veteran salespeople are more likely to justify their slowed initiative as a reward for years of successful selling.

Poor initiative is a learned negative habit to a sales-contact opportunity. People seldom decide consciously to avoid their own customers. Many poor producers aren't even aware of what we call *contact hesitation*. Here are three ways to check if your applicant has initiative or contact hesitation.

1. Probe for bad selling experiences.

   Even with people who have never had a sales job, ask about what he liked or didn't like when he had to sell candy or magazine subscriptions or whatever it was for school fundraisers. Did the fundraiser contact neighbors and friends to buy, or did Mom and Dad end up buying the inventory? If they didn't sell then, chances are pretty good they aren't going to sell now without a lot of intervention.

2. Ask about ways the candidate is comfortable or uncomfortable contacting prospects.

   Contact hesitation attaches itself to certain types of sales contacts. If you use any of these approaches to find customers, you will want to explore and identify any emotional barriers to any or all of the following:
   - telephone prospecting (people who hate telemarketers don't want to be perceived as one)
   - canvassing (door-to-door cold calling may be considered demeaning)
   - networking (using one's personal sphere of influence to develop business leads may trigger the hesitation to put some people off-limits to prospecting)
   - asking for referrals (some salespeople hesitate for fear of jeopardizing the current sale or appearing pushy)
   - contacting clientele outside of one's socioeconomic group (some individuals may feel uncomfortable with wealthy clientele like doctors or lawyers)

- making presentations to groups of people (not likely to happen if your candidate suffers from acute stage fright)

Although the salesperson will try to make it sound rational, avoidance issues are usually more emotional in nature.

Josh is an example of rationalizing one's contact hesitation. He is a sales manager for a real estate business. When Josh was in sales he hated using the telephone. "It's just better to make the personal contact," Josh said. "They can't say no to you as easily."

Now as a manager Josh discourages his agents from using the phone except for the most mundane activities. "If it's important, it should be face-to-face," Josh insists.

Josh has institutionalized his emotional barrier toward phone sales. He would probably disagree with us if we were to tell him that he's actually making the contact hesitation of his agents worse. He thinks he's improving initiative by forcing more face-to-face cold calls. But Josh's office has fewer listings than other offices in his city, and his team's results suffer.

Remember, the most successful salespeople do not hesitate to use all available and appropriate methods to approach business opportunities. Poor performers have hang-ups about making certain kinds of sales calls that they have turned into habits that pilfer their productivity by undermining their initiative.

3. Delay recontacting an applicant.

We think the best way to evaluate a candidate's initiative (short of giving them the SalesKey assessment) is for the recruiter to delay getting back in touch with a job prospect. This will demand that if the person is really interested in the job, he or she will have to take some initiative to call you back. Our experience is that most people will call back once, but postponing your conversation so that your candidate must make two or three attempts to reach you becomes an excellent predictor of initiative. This is one of the reasons why it's so important not to be in a hurry to hire.

Trying to meet deadlines can take away important tactics by which you can evaluate the productivity potential of your sales candidates.

Although there are proven ways to help sales reps deal with contact hesitation, the best approach is to do everything you can to not hire people with poor initiative. Select the people who love to prospect and who enjoy the hunt as much as they enjoy the result of the hunt. Interviewees will always respond positively regarding their desire to prospect, because anyone interviewing for a sales role knows that prospecting is foundational to the job. However, many times in their desire to get a job, people with contact hesitation assume that they'll be able to change the prospecting formula and make it work. All too frequently it doesn't work, and the typical outcome is subpar performance and managerial headaches for month after month as the manager works to get the low initiative salesperson off the bus.

6. BALANCED PRAGMATISM

We've added this behavior to the second edition of *Hire Performance* to cover a key ingredient found primarily in determining the capacity of the strategic sales candidate and secondarily of all types of salespeople. Balanced pragmatism refers to the degree to which a salesperson will sacrifice self-interest to benefit the customer or the team. Now all types of selling require basic integrity, since trust is foundational to every relationship. Employers need to know that their salespeople are doing what is best for the company and for its customer rather than offering unneeded products or services because the commission may be higher or because of some other benefit that accrues to the sales rep.

We have witnessed subtle but definite erosion in the ethical standards of workers over the past twenty years. To some degree this is due to the pervasiveness of postmodern ideas; namely, that there is no such thing as objective truth, and that what is right for you may not be right for me. Another dimension of this growing cultural pragmatism is the global economy and the liberalizing influence of multiculturalism on social groups whose values were previously monolithic. Values once taken for granted are now questioned and overturned. For example, there are still some sales professions in which women salespeople are the exception rather than the rule. Racial stereotypes once considered the norm are no longer tolerated. Newspaper headlines scream about venerable and trusted companies caught lying and cheating their customers and the taxpayers. In times of cultural change, it's not surprising that strict adherence to standards may be considered old-fashioned and quaint.

Résumés today can be exercises in creative writing. We estimate on the basis of our conversations with recruiters that as many as one third of résumés will contain a significant attempt at some degree of subterfuge. There are two common breaches of integrity:

1. Reason for leaving previous employer
2. Salary history

How is a recruiter to cope with this crisis of integrity when references are reluctant to say anything that could be negatively construed and therefore leave them open them to a possible lawsuit? Here are some behavioral cues that indicate that someone may be less than honest in their answer.

- Touching or rubbing the nose, while not always an indication of someone telling a lie, is frequently the body language of deception.
- Another tell can be the stiffness of one's posture and the lack of gestures. The more anxious people become under the stress of telling a lie, the more likely they are to freeze up as a way of self-protection.
- Verbally, people who are dishonest can sometimes come across as just too good to be true.
- Anyone who says, "Let me be honest with you," probably isn't.
- Overly pragmatic people may have a habit of overstating things or adding qualifiers that give them escape routes from responsibility. For example, words like think, might, could, maybe, perhaps, potentially, possibly, but, and the biggest

powerless word of all—try. When people talk, listen for these indicators of taking a shortcut around responsibility.

It's possible that people can be too rigid as well, like Brian, a former US Marine who went to work as a stockbroker. He was a stickler for doing things by the book. His employer was running a special promotion; any client who moved a certain dollar volume of assets into a new account by a specific date would receive a new titanium golf club. One of Brian's clients had actually exceeded the promotional limit substantially, adding several million dollars to a new account. When he called Brian to ask when he might be receiving his golf club, Brian said, "Sorry, sir. I'm afraid you missed the cutoff for that promotion by a day."

When the client threatened to reverse his decision and take back his millions, Brian's manager made sure the golf club was sent by overnight express. Brian may have been correct, but there can be situations in which a balanced pragmatic approach to the rules and regulations should be maintained.

CONCLUSION

Six behaviors make up Level 1 and are the nontrainable foundation for predicting the effort and capacity of any candidate for hard work and success.

1. Energy represents how hard someone will work.
2. Goal motivation is the drive to achieve.
3. A positive sales identity means that selling is a career the individual values.
4. Balanced risk sensitivity points to someone who can manage some instability without becoming preoccupied with worry.
5. Initiative is approaching people and situations that develop opportunities rather than avoiding them.
6. A balanced pragmatism is necessary to any relationship of trust between company, customer, and salesperson.

7

TWO BEHAVIORS OF LEVEL 2

You can hire a salesperson with great energy, goal motivation, sales identity, balanced risk sensitivity, initiative, and balanced pragmatism and still not have a productive rep if the company's managers don't know how to coach or the company's products are not competitive or product training is subpar. After validating foundation behaviors of Level 1 and knowing if your prospect can and will sell, you must next begin looking for Level 2 clues about how efficiently this candidate will be able to sell. You need to know whether there are going to be additional training and management costs associated with hiring this individual.

Someone without any sales experience is going to cost a business considerably more to get up to speed than someone who has relevant experience. This is the major reason employers look for experienced candidates—to minimize Level 2 training and development costs as well as to get a quicker return on their recruitment costs. But previous experience can sometimes be detrimental. If a former employer renamed the sales function to "consultant" or "relationship engineer," you're likely to inherit someone with a weak sales identity. Sales veterans may have gone through sales-training programs that are incompatible with the kind of selling done in your firm. Very seldom do we hear recruiters ask candidates about the kind of sales training they may have been exposed to in their previous job. Someone coming out of a strong one-call close sales environment may represent more Level 2 costs to a company that uses a consultative-sales approach. The toll is even higher if someone is coming the other way—from consultative selling into a hard-sell culture. That is a very difficult transition.

Are you recruiting college graduates? Then you'd better have a strong sales-training program and a dynamic manager's coaching program, because college grads drive up Level 2 costs with not only their need for professional sales training but also their expectations of quality instruction. The same holds true for individuals leaving companies with strong training programs. They are going to expect and require recruitment perks beyond merely the base package and commission rate, all of which drives up the cost of recruitment and requires a greater return on investment.

Hiring experienced reps also means you could be recruiting someone else's problem. If things were going as great as the résumé says, what are the chances that this candidate is even looking for another job? Sure, lots of people move on for a better opportunity, but Hire Performance demands that you look beyond the clichés of self-promoters to what actually prompted a candidate's decision to move on. There are seven cognitive measures in a SalesKey Level 2 profile. But you can evaluate the two most important without the questionnaire. These are cognitive skills that directly impact sales efficiency.

1. PROBLEM SOLVING

Today selling is about designing solutions for customers. Globalization has meant increased competition. Online shopping has turned price into a commodity. Salespeople today have to sell value. Brands may use advertising to manipulate the perception of value, but one appliance is probably just as good as another; insurance is a commodity because the costs are regulated by states. Discount brokers compete to see who can drop the price of trades the most because trades have become a commodity. So, if you have competitors who sell essentially the same product or service and sometimes at the same price, the only way the salesperson can add value is to specifically link up a product or service customized to meet a specific consumer need. When Ma Bell was the telephone monopoly she could charge you whatever she wanted. But with deregulation in the mid-1980s, the telephone industry changed forever. Competition forced down prices and created lots of new options. The winning companies were those with salespeople who could tailor-make just the right solution.

We are convinced that twenty-first-century selling requires good-to-excellent problem-solving skills. Although intelligence can be a plus, what you're looking for in a sales candidate is patience with complexity. The marketplace has become much more complex. In the last century choices were more limited than today. Henry Ford once said, "You can have a Model T in any color as long as it is black." Today Ford doesn't make only one model in one color but lots of models in a rainbow of colors, competing with lots of models from lots of other car companies. Making a sale requires asking good questions, listening to what the prospect says, and designing a solution to capture the imagination or ease the pain of the customer.

We witnessed this fact firsthand when asked to consult with a national coffee company. For years this venerable firm sold plain and simple coffee, what they call in the industry "hot and black" brands. Coffee was coffee. It was a commodity sale, and the only problem solving required by salespeople was finding out what the customer was paying for their current brand and coming up with a better price. The coffee business was pretty simple until Starbucks changed everything. Sales at the traditional coffee company fell as a new generation of coffee drinkers switched to gourmet coffee and local roasters. A new VP of sales caught the vision that salespeople needed to stop selling the commodity and begin thinking of coffee in a new way. He hired us to help these veteran coffee salespeople stop quoting prices and start asking questions and designing solutions. We worked for two years on this goal, but it was a lost cause. Long-tenured salespeople rejected the approach. Frustrated by the failure of his sales force to meet the challenge of a new generation of coffee drinkers, the visionary VP left to work for the soft-drink industry. Today the coffee firm is no longer in business.

In our research, we find consistently strong correlations between an individual's problem-solving ability and his or her ability to succeed in designing solutions for customers from many available options.

Buy a book of brain teasers or Mensa puzzles. If you are using an assessment that does not measure problem-solving skills, include a dozen nonword problems as a supplement to your employment application. Word problems have been found to be discriminatory in some situations. So you want to use problems that do not rely on words but instead use graphics or numbers. For example, look for the kind of problems that present a series of shapes or a group of objects from which the candidate must determine either the next pattern in a sequence or the relationship between objects. Remember, you're not necessarily looking for a genius but for an individual with the patience to sort through a variety of options and think clearly enough to arrive at a solution. If the applicant spends too much time trying to solve a problem, this may indicate that he or she is going to have difficulties closing sales quickly or generating options for customers. If your candidate gets the answer wrong, that's not a disaster.

Some years ago we were experimenting with some new questions for our assessment. We were looking for an item that would detect unconventional thinking. So we came up with this statement with which the respondent was to agree or disagree: "I can imagine a six-sided square." We thought sane people would answer no, since by definition squares have four sides. We were surprised when one individual in our sample actually answered yes to the item. He happened to be someone we knew to be very intelligent.

"How can you imagine a six-sided square?" we wanted to know.

"Easy," he said, "it's a cube."

We could quibble about the meaning of words, or we could understand that someone people can see solutions in a way most folks can't. So if someone gets one of your problems wrong, ask how he or she tried to solve the problem. If it's clear that the applicant more or less guessed at an answer without thinking it through, you're looking at a potential Level 2 problem, especially if your firm sells a complex product line, expects a long sales cycle, or educates buyers in a technical product or service, or if you are trying to differentiate yourself from competitors on the basis of your salespeople becoming valued business partners.

Poor problem solvers make for inefficient salespeople in two principle ways:

1. They may not sell the full line of company products and services. People with poor problem-solving skills find one or two products that they master fairly well and ignore other options they may not completely understand. This not only may limit productivity but may mean that customers are apt to be presented with something that isn't really a match to their need but fits the salesperson's limitations. As the old proverb says, "If your only tool is a hammer, everything looks like a nail."

2. They're more likely to make mistakes that cost the company time, money, and customers. This is the direct consequence of trying to sell customers what the rep likes to sell rather than what the customer wants or needs. This leads not only to mistakes but to irritated customers and the loss of brand equity.

2. FOCUS

Another important cognitive function that impacts sales productivity is the ability to focus attention on what is important and not become distracted by peripheral diversions. Think for a moment about how critical one's ability to focus is to training. Will the individual be able to pay attention in classroom settings? Can your potential rep handle the complexity of technical products and sales? If you have an extensive product line, will this salesperson find it difficult to recommend the right solutions for customers, or will a lack of focus increase mistakes and foster a tendency to jump on the first thing a prospect says and miss out on drilling down to deeper issues? In lean economic times when businesses are forced to cut back, salespeople may need to pick up additional tasks once performed by other staff. Salespeople with poor focus will cost the firm money because with the increased workload they frequently lose sight of high payoff priorities. These are just a few ways that poor focus lowers productivity. Reps with poor focus tend to do poorly in training and increase management costs considerably.

Sometimes poor focus is the problem of the individual. So much is written today about the problem of attention deficit disorder. According to the Centers for Disease Control, nearly 9 percent of young people have been diagnosed with the condition. ADD is about twice as prevalent in boys as girls. These people have problems with concentration because they lose focus easily. As these young people enter the job market, the problem is only going to get worse. The information age and smart phones provide not only ubiquitous interruptions from tweets, texts, and calls but also nearly unlimited instant diversion at the first twinge of boredom.

But more often than not, a lack of focus isn't merely the fault of the individual employee but of the organization itself. Salespeople get unfocused by the nefarious flavor-of-the-month administrative initiative. Companies roll out program after program, many of which may contradict each other and all of them expensive, in an effort to spend the training budget on the latest fad or buzz. Salespeople start down one direction only to be yanked away into another program. Many employment ads ask for people who can "multitask in a fast-paced work environment." This can often be code for an organization without a clear focus, lurching from one initiative to another initiative without long-term insight into how their multiplied training offerings actually create a culture of cynics. Cynicism is the final coping strategy for people in a goal-diffused and unfocused organization.

Take the example of a national financial services company that hired us to improve the productivity of their reps through both our Hire Performance program and our coaching of existing salespeople. We had many Level 1 issues to address, such as poor sales identity and the lack of meaningful goals. At Level 2 the overall focus of the sales force was horrible. The company had created one of those online learning universities for employees with hundreds of course options. Don't get us wrong—there's nothing wrong with providing a rich training environment. But without a cohesive sales platform all the options became confusing escape routes for reps with contact hesitation who didn't want to make prospecting calls. We started at the beginning with Level 1 behaviors and a laser-like focus on unlocking energy with meaningful goals so salespeople could and would take the initiative to make more contacts. The payoff was enormous. We measured productivity by the number of reps who were hitting their sales targets versus the number who were below their quota. In spite of a downturn in the stock market, nearly three times as many reps were hitting their targets as were prior to our engagement. We managed to hold off the training department's desire to lurch from program to program for about a year. But then a new CEO came onboard, brought in his own people, undermined our science of sales with a well-known program featuring a soft approach, and promptly dismissed us. Next quarter, sales were in the tank, where they have remained for years, even after this same company spent $5,000,000 on yet another training program that has provided virtually no lift at all. Salespeople don't use it, while their competitor, with whom we have been working for a number of years, has eclipsed them in every aspect of measured sales productivity.

From a recruiting perspective, it doesn't matter how your candidates train their brain to be more distracted than focused. Sales productivity requires people paying attention to first-rate priorities first.

Here are five ways to spot poor focus in your interview with a candidate.

1. Poor time-management skills. The problem with a loss of focus is the inability to distinguish priorities. Ask if your candidate has ever had time-management training and whether she still uses what she learned. Time management is usually a waste of time with people who have focus issues. They readily admit the importance of the skill but have great difficulty practicing it. If your applicant was late for the interview, this should be a red flag unless the person can give a very good reason for the tardiness. Habitual lateness and missing deadlines is a marker behavior for low focus.

2. Do you hear non sequitur answers to your questions? Poor focus means people sometimes miss out on what is being said by something that momentarily distracts them. None of us likes to be distracted in an interview, but you should learn to use any distraction to your benefit. Can the applicant pick up the conversation from the point before the interruption? If the applicant has to ask you to repeat a question or says, "I've

forgotten what I was saying," this may be an indication that they have difficulty concentrating on what's important.

3. Ask about previous training programs. Did their current or previous employer have a flavor-of-the-month approach? If the candidate says yes, drill down on his or her attitude toward the parade of programs. Ask if some of the programs contradicted each other. This may help identify someone who has been better trained to be a cynic than how to be an effective sales rep. It's important that you determine what sales-training programs the individual remembers and actually uses in selling, if any. How much do his or her current assumptions align with your priorities?

4. Check the applicant's social media. As we will discuss in a later chapter, you should check out the candidate's Twitter feed and Facebook postings. The more deeply involved your potential hire is with social media, the more likely he or she may be prone to distraction. Another clue, of course, is to listen for the telltale hum of a smart phone set to vibrate. Of course, interrupting your job interview to take a call is a dead giveaway.

5. Ask about boredom. What does your candidate do if and when bored? How much inactivity can the person tolerate? Ask if he takes out his smart phone when in the middle of conversations with friends and others. If so, expect focus issues.

CONCLUSION

Once salespeople are hired, your company invests time and money to train them. Recruiting a winning sales team requires evaluating two behaviors that are associated with Level 2 efficiency in the sales process:

1. Problem solving—the ability to create customized solutions for customers' unique needs

2. Focus—the capacity to know what's important and what's not and deter distractions

These cognitive skills of your potential hire will enable you to get a rapid and complete return on the investment of the firm's training dollars.

8

LEVEL 3: A MODEL FOR EFFECTIVE COMMUNICATION

So far we've examined two of the Four Levels of Sales: Level 1 contained six behaviors that determine the effort and the capacity of an individual to perform the essential skills of a sales position. Level 2 focused on two cognitive skills that increase the efficiency of the sales rep. Let's turn next to Level 3—a model for understanding the effectiveness of the candidate's communication to influence sales interactions. Does he talk more than he listens? Does she unearth customer needs or excel at show-and-tell sales presentations? Is he cold and alienating or warm and accepting? What kinds of prospects or customers seem difficult for her to close? Why are some people bubbly and others unenthusiastic? Why do some people have such a hard time closing while others seem to undersell (going for the close without a buying signal)? Remember, the behavior you see in the job interview is probably someone putting his or her best foot forward. A recruiter needs a model (sometimes called a paradigm) for knowing how this person is likely to behave in real sales interactions after getting the job. Here are four behavioral models making the rounds in the marketplace today that attempt to answer the question "Why do people do what they do?"

PERSONALITY MODELS

Most recruiters assume that they are looking for people with an extroverted personality; that is, individuals who are outgoing and social. Quiet, shy introverts get weeded out of the sales search early on in favor of glib, back-slapping bon vivants. But today there are so many more opportunities for people other than the glad-handing, life-of-the-party type of sales reps. A lot of firms want someone who doesn't tell jokes but asks questions; doesn't shoot the breeze but designs solutions; isn't looking for the fast buck but adds value to gain a larger share of the wallet. It's more cerebral today. We now know that people categorized as introverts by personality can actually do quite well in the right kind of sales environment. People do not have to try to change their personalities to improve their productivity; and that's a good thing, because people are born with their personalities, and those attributes are relatively fixed for life.

BEHAVIORIST MODEL

Another way of looking at behavior is the behaviorist model. This approach says that people are simple stimulus-and-response mechanisms. We approach things we get rewarded for and avoid things we get punished for. Programs driven by this philosophy say it's up to the organization to shape the desired behavior of its salespeople. This model underlies all competency-based programs: break the job down into its component behaviors and then find ways to incentivize salespeople to perform those behaviors. Think of a rat in a maze. Every time it makes the correct move, throw in a piece of cheese.

In this model, the recruiter looks at people primarily in terms of their experience with specific past behaviors as well as past salary history and compares the candidate to the offer being made by the company. But what if the company doesn't know the competencies, or what if they are the wrong competencies? What if most of the pay package is commission or bonus? These undermine the applicability of the approach.

There are other serious problems with a purely behaviorist approach to sales. After seeing a study we did in which the highest-producing salespeople made the most contacts, one of our Fortune 500 clients decided that they would incentivize this behavior; that is, salespeople would earn a bonus based on how many people they met and talked to. The result was disastrous. The company saw lots of new contact activity, but the number of sales actually decreased significantly. It turned out that salespeople were padding their contact numbers with phony activity. Instead of making more presentations and proposals, reps did only what they were incentivized for and not much else: run up contact numbers. When the incentive program was scrapped, the same salespeople actually made fewer contacts than before the behaviorist experiment. Alfie Kohn, in his book *Punished by Rewards: The Trouble with Gold Stars, Incentive Plans, A's, Praise, and Other Bribes*, says that whatever behavior you incentivize will actually decrease over time if you don't continue increasing the what's-in-it-for-me factor. So productivity gets held hostage by the comp plan. The fact that salespeople cheated the system is one of the ugly hidden assumptions behind a behaviorist model: there is no right and wrong, only what the higher-ups want rewarded or punished.

When we talk about looking at behaviors, we want to emphasize we are not behaviorists. We are not advocating shaping behavior with bribes. This totally contradicts our recruitment strategy statement (see chapter 4).

THIRD-FORCE MODEL

Another way of looking at behavior is the third-force model. Behaviorism was a reaction to the poor success rates of Freudian psychoanalysis to modify behavior. Freud and Behaviorists were the first two forces in the field. Then along came Abraham Maslow and Carl Rogers and others who stressed the uniqueness and goodness of every individual. According to third-force theorists, you help people articulate their problems as they see them, encourage them to develop goals, and support them as they pursue the way that seems best to them in achieving those goals. Third force is all about what the individual wants, not what a therapist or supervisor wants. It is nondirective, because the Third-Force model says that people know what is best for them and how to achieve it.

This model has become quite popular in sales circles repackaged as "consultation selling" or "client-centered selling." The salesperson is little more than a well-trained prompt to get the customer talking about problems and solutions. In consultation selling, you don't close sales; you open relationships. In client-centered selling, the sales rep is a facilitator of the customer's desires and operates only on the customer's timetable.

The third-force model is not without its problems as well. Its customer-centered approach was designed and first implemented by manufacturing businesses building customized systems for other large businesses. We think a third-force model has some merit for similar organizations that engage primarily in strategic sales. But our experience is that many direct-sales companies rolled out the consultation model as the latest fad and to cover for the lack of leadership provided by sales management. Those businesses have seen sales plummet as salespeople become little more than professional visitors. If your salespeople are expected to make a certain number of sales each month to sell company products and services, the strategic selling model will bankrupt you. Waiting for customers to tell you when they are ready to buy only increases the cost of sales and diminishes volume by significantly slowing down the sales process.

Here's an example of what happens when a business changes their behavior model to this approach.

Brandon was one recruiter who had read lots of books about the winning personalities of great salespeople. He visited other sales recruiters and learned that successful salespeople possessed drive and passion and the ability to close. He was hiring Type A "hunters," as one author has referred to them. However, the firm's sales training was changed to a program based on a third-force model, emphasizing listening, patience, and analyzing customer needs. Brandon couldn't understand why his top candidates became dissatisfied and washed out after six months, especially those with proven track records of closing a lot of sales. It didn't take us long to figure out what was going on. Brandon was recruiting people based on their aggressiveness, but the training department was using a customer-centered training approach and was in effect trying to put that square peg in a round hole.

BARNETT'S INTEGRATED MODEL

Dr. Barnett developed the integrated behavioral model more than twenty years ago to allow recruiting and training to work from a single set of assumptions about behavior. This model integrates some aspects of the behaviorist model and some elements of the Third-Force model. We look at behaviors in order to infer customer needs. Hire Performance Level 3 is built upon Barnett's integrated model. Level 3 allows us to not only *de*scribe behaviors, but we can also *pre*scribe what to do with that information to make one a more effective communicator. Our model is not perfect, and some academics might consider it overly simplified, but it has proven time and time again to be both accurate *enough* and easy to use on the fly in actual conversations. Using this model, you can tell within ten seconds of starting most conversations what the prevailing emotional needs of an individual might be. Knowing those needs allows you to meet those needs and thereby directly influence the sales decision.

Simply put, Barnett's integrated model says that people develop patterns of behavior in order to satisfy emotional needs. These patterns become habits and can be described as "styles." You and the people you interview and whom you seek to influence are all behaving in accordance with a style of interaction with which they and you have become comfortable. A person comes to you looking for a job. She has a business need; she's seeking employment. But she also has emotional needs that will shape how she communicates with you about that business need. Those same preferences will shape her communication with everyone else as well, including future managers and customers. If you want to influence her to accept your offer, you will need to meet both the business need and the emotional needs that drive the customer's communication style.

In years of research with SalesKey and other assessments, Dr. Barnett isolated five emotional needs that can be detected in the majority of sales and service interactions:

- need for stability
- need for control
- need for attention
- need for approval
- need for information

You've already encountered the need for stability in Level 1, what we called risk sensitivity. This emotional need is placed at Level 1 because it applies primarily to effort and capacity more than to communication effectiveness.

When you know the individual's emotional needs and know how to meet those needs, you put yourself in a strong position of influence. Level 2 is about our efficiency in meeting the business needs of customers: matching the features and benefits of the right product to the expressed need of the buyer. Level 2 business needs tend to be logical, but the emotional needs that make up Level 3 tend to be personal, unexamined, and often more than a little irrational. To say these needs are emotional doesn't mean they make us emotional. In some cases emotional needs can actually cut off a person from his or her emotions. We refer to them as emotional because they are not rational and thought out.

These habits of style become so routine and so automatic that we don't think about them. We say that's just the way we are, because for as long as we can remember that's how we have interacted with others.

CONCLUSION

Recruiters need an understanding of behavior. In this chapter we've described four different models that recruiters might use.

1. Personality theory is the traditional approach to sales recruiting; look for extroverted personalities, but personality is fixed and difficult to change.
2. Behaviorist theory says people do what they get rewarded to do, but this approach puts others in control of people's lives and can be amoral.
3. Third-Force theory underlies much of the customer-centered approaches that can be disastrous for direct sales by slowing down the sales process.
4. Barnett's integrated model is an eclectic combination of behaviorist and customer-centric approaches that infers needs by observing behaviors.

9

FOUR EMOTIONAL NEEDS OF LEVEL 3

Everything we do is to satisfy some desire, drive, or appetite of which we may or may not be aware. We all have preferred ways of interacting with others. We don't think about these preferences in relationships; they are automatic and not always rational, which is why we refer to them as emotional needs.

Emotional needs are:

1. **Innate**. Everyone is born with all five emotional needs. Each is essential for survival and growth as a human being. During our maturation, we learn that having some of these needs met is more pleasurable than other needs. So some needs may come to dominate behavior, but not to the exclusion of all others.
2. **Universal**. There is no cultural bias in the Level 3 model. Although some cultures may place a higher value on some social behaviors than others, emotional needs are present in every ethnic group in the world. The universality of these emotional needs are validated in our cross-cultural studies and administering our assessment around the world.
3. **Intuitive**. These behaviors are acquired very early in life, some even prenatally. By early childhood some emotional

needs may come to dominate others based on repetition and reinforcement.

4. **Dynamic**. The relative strength of needs may shift within an individual depending on a role or a specific environment. For example, the need for control may dominate someone at work, but when around one's spouse and children that need may become less influential than the need for attention.

At their most basic level, emotional needs shape what we approach and what we avoid in social relationships. Satisfying any of these four needs releases dopamine in the brain and causes feelings of pleasure and well-being. The reward power of satisfying these needs is very strong and develops habits that can last a lifetime. Being starved of any of these emotional needs helps create phobias, dislikes, and fears. These preferences and habits strongly influence how we make decisions, including how we like to buy. Some people always have to think it over, while others are impulse buyers. Why is this so? Because some folks get pats on the back for being smart, while others get rewarded for being spontaneous. Some people want a strong relational component to a sale, while others prefer to be left alone with the facts to decide. Why? Some people have developed strong intuitive feelings about people, and others have been burned by enough people to know you can't trust anyone. Emotional needs drive our interactions.

EMOTIONAL NEEDS HAVE THREE STATES

The question invariably arises, "What's the best kind of salesperson to recruit?" Since everyone has all four of these Level 3 emotional needs, what we have found is that the most successful salespeople tend to have all four emotional needs in what we call *a state of balance*. This means that all four emotional needs are being satisfied to a degree that the individual can adapt his or her style to the emotional needs of others.

Emotional needs exist in three states as they impact communication. Each emotional need can be:

1. **Balanced**. This is the optimum condition, when an emotional need is neither too strong nor too weak. The style is not dominating one's behavior to the exclusion of one or more emotional needs. We believe that when a person's emotional need is being met, this frees up energy and focus so that the salesperson can focus on adapting his or her style to the needs of customers. The typical sales conversation requires that the salesperson adapt one's self-presentation in order to effectively communicate.

2. **High Unbalanced**. When a particular emotional need is dominating the others, certain behaviors will exercise more influence on a person's social style in order to satisfy that drive. Identifying these behaviors enables us to infer the emotional need. As the emotional need gets more out of balance, the salesperson is likely to be less productive. The clusters of behaviors that accompany the high-unbalanced style become the names we give to the out-of-balance condition. For example, a controller is someone with a high-unbalanced need for control. We call someone with a high-unbalanced need for information an *analyzer*. When someone has a strong unmet emotional need for approval, we talk about the *empathizer* style. The person with the high-unbalanced need for attention is called a *performer* style. These labels are meant to be nonpejorative. Each has strengths, but each also has limitations.

3. **Underbalanced**. This is the state of an emotional need that should be exerting more influence than it currently does. The individual may not even be aware of the need and how it can impact productivity. Underbalanced needs are called *avoidant* styles. A low approval need creates a series of behaviors that are approval avoidant. The approval-avoidant salesperson may intentionally alienate customers or team members or be completely unconcerned with what others may think. It is very difficult to assess the avoidant styles because each is a mirror opposite one of the emotional needs. For example, the

behaviors of the approval-avoidant rep look very similar to the high-unbalanced control style, but the motivation is completely different. One is trying to avoid something, and the other is trying to approach something. Consequently, in this book we are going to focus primarily on the balanced and high-unbalanced states.

Let's look at the behaviors associated with the balanced and high-unbalanced state of the emotional needs as they occur in the typical sequence of a sales conversation.

THE NEED FOR APPROVAL

Shortly after the attention stage of the sales conversation, the salesperson must begin asking questions and listening to what the customer is saying and feeling. Every sales process ever devised includes a relationship-building stage as the salesperson stops chatting and starts asking questions about what is important to the customer. Salespeople with a balanced approval need are relationally astute. They are excellent listeners and know how to make people comfortable with them. The balanced approval need allows salespeople to be comfortable with the give-and-take of conversation. Successful salespeople also possess an "accurate empathy"—the innate ability to sense where they are in a relationship at any given point. Does the customer like me? Accept me? Trust me? In other words, are we ready to do business? Top producers work from a balanced approval need that allows the customer to feel important to the salesperson.

Empathizers are salespeople with a strong unbalanced approval need. Relational sensitivity has become relational dependence. Because empathizers irrationally believe that everyone should like them, they become overly accommodating with customers. They are uncomfortable closing sales or asking for referrals because they fear losing the approval of the prospect or client. They are notoriously indecisive because they will always check to see what others are thinking before they commit to anything. They struggle to get beyond visiting with customers and prospects to actually doing business with them. In one study with the coffee company we mentioned earlier, we found a high correlation between salespeople's empathizer scores and the number of samples given away to prospects. High-approval-need individuals use gifts to secure the approval of others. Empathizers excel at customer service. It's not unusual for a strong out-of-balance approval need to drive salespeople to take the side of their customers against their own companies.

Empathizers usually make lousy salespeople in direct sales but are often some of the very best customer-service people. In study after study, the poorest salespeople are those who fear rejection and require that their prospects never feel the pressure of their influence. They are most uncomfortable with the close and wait for the customer to tell them when they are ready to buy.

If the approval need is too low, salespeople don't care what others think about them and may be impatient and utterly uncaring about the relational aspects of the sale. Approval avoidance is a serious barrier to communication. It motivates those under its influence to push people away and be needlessly confrontational. We will address this more fully when we talk about the high-unbalanced need for control, as that is how you will most easily spot this behavior.

Table 1 summarizes the three states of the emotional need for approval.

Balanced Approval Need	High Approval Need (Empathizer Style)	Low Approval Need (Approval-Avoidant Style)
• is relationally sensitive • builds rapport well • is an active listener • services the sale	• is accommodating • fears being rejected by client • won't close sales • is indecisive	• is oppositional • doesn't care what others think • has behaviors similar to controller

Table 1

THE NEED FOR INFORMATION

After building rapport, the typical sales conversation moves to the probing stage, asking questions and developing a plan to solve a customer's problems. Good salespeople have lots of information at their fingertips about how products and services help meet customers' needs. The emotional need for information, when balanced, allows people to match features and benefits and calculate the ROI of any potential proposal. Good salespeople are comfortable planning and working with details without becoming nitpicking perfectionists.

When the emotional need for information goes unfulfilled and begins to exert more influence on behavior than other emotional needs, productivity suffers. We call the salespeople with a high-unbalanced need for information *analyzers*. They are the bean counters. They slow down the sales process by the "paralysis of analysis." Analyzers seldom feel adequately prepared for their calls. Yes, they give the impression of being workaholics, but their unbalanced need for more and more data just makes them put in longer hours in an effort to feel prepared. Analyzers may do quite well at some types of selling, such as high-tech sales. Of all the selling styles, the high-unbalanced-information need exerts the least effect on sales productivity. But for most direct sales, skills like planning, organizing, and analyzing are only part of the sales process.

At the other extreme, information-avoidant reps can't be bothered with too much information. They sell by the KISS motto—"Keep it short and simple." Downplaying analysis, they prefer intuitive decision making. These information-avoidant individuals act very much like the performer. Both are impatient with details. Both expect quick fixes. But the motivation is completely different. In the selection process, it's enough to recognize the general nature of an out-of-balance situation to help you predict the behavior issues you may face with customers and others members of the team.

Table 2 summarizes the three states of the information need.

Balanced Information Need	High Information Need (Analyzer Style)	Low Information Need (Information-Avoidant Style)
• plans well • is a problem solver • excels at product knowledge	• is a perfectionist • is a workaholic • nitpicks • never feels adequately prepared	• is intuitive • gets impatient with details • expects quick fixes to problems

Table 2

THE NEED FOR CONTROL

A sale is a relationship. A sale is an opportunity to show off both problem-solving and communication skills, but ultimately a decision must be made by the customer and money must change hands. Top performers know that they have to close the sale. At some point in the conversation, show-and-tell ceases, rapport-building ends, and problem solving and product knowledge take a back seat as the salesperson steps into a position of control and tries to influence an outcome. Selling usually involves some degree of assertion. Those who do it best have a balanced control need. They are comfortable overcoming objections and consequently are probably effective at making a lot of sales.

When the emotional need for control is overactive, the person's communication style is called the controller. The controller needs to always be dominant in the relationship, and when he or she is not in that role, the controller can become argumentative and even intimidating of team members and customers alike. Someone who tries to overcontrol the sales process is often impatient with social niceties. The controller gets to the bottom line quickly and will try to close even if there's not a clear buy signal. And the controller may keep on closing a sale as many times as it takes to impose his or her will on the customer.

Controllers tend to be lone wolves. They don't like working on teams, because teams can be very inefficient. Teamwork also demands shared ownership of ideas, and that's just not something controllers do comfortably.

Because they are comfortable with power and are excellent decision makers, controllers tend to work their way to the top of the power hierarchy within companies. When this happens, their values and behaviors become the norm and can influence the entire sales culture. In the controller sales culture, reps are trained to not accept no for an answer. If the customer doesn't move quickly enough to a decision, the controller may issue the client an ultimatum ("If you don't buy this today, the discount goes away") or even question the customer's integrity or ability.

People with a high emotional need for control are often attracted to sales because they are results-driven individuals, extremely task oriented. However, customer care often takes a back seat to winning with controllers. Extremely competitive, controllers may alienate customers who prefer a more relational approach to the sale.

At the other end of the control spectrum are reps who don't take enough control of the sales process. They defer to clients. The control-avoidant salesperson waits for the customer to say when he or she is ready to buy. Since most customers don't do this, low control salespeople make fewer sales. In many ways, their behaviors mimic those of the empathizer, but the motivation is different. Empathizers are trying to win approval; control-avoidant individuals just want someone else to make the decision.

Table 3 summarizes the states of the control need.

Balanced Control Need	High Control Need (the Controller Style)	Low Control Need (Control Avoidant)
• is decisive • takes control of the sales process • easily handles objections • is self-directed	• is opinionated and critical • is not a team player • may be intimidating • fears losing control • may go for the close too early	• is deferring • prefers to let others control the relationship • is dependent • has behaviors similar to high approval need

Table 3

You will come across candidates from time to time who seem to exhibit being out of balance on three and occasionally all four of these needs. Our experience is that these are intense individuals who are very competitive. This can be beneficial in achieving spectacular sales results. The key is once these intensive individuals are hired, you must move quickly to leverage the good that comes with their intensity and mitigate the behaviors that can limit them from maximizing their full potential.

THE BALANCED SALESPERSON

As a recruiter, you're looking for someone who is a good planner (analyzer) *and* considerate (empathizer) *and* self-controlled (controller) *and* confident (performer). From our analysis of thousands of salespeople, about a fifth of salespeople fit this description. They sell more because they are able to adapt their own behavior to match the relational, communication, analytical, and power sensitivities of differing communication styles.

This can be represented graphically (see figure 2). Proximity to the center represents the balanced state of the emotional needs. But as a particular need becomes unbalanced to the high side, notice how the behaviors become less and less productive. So, for example, the empathizer becomes hesitant and uncommitted and the controller negative and bossy.

Remember, these same styles operate in recruiters as well. Recruiters are going to make more and better placements when they can learn to recognize these styles in their candidates and adapt their recruiting behaviors to match the traits and preferences of the salespeople they are trying to attract. In the next chapter, we provide you with the clues to recognizing the communication styles and give you some basic guidance on how to meet their emotional as well as their business needs.

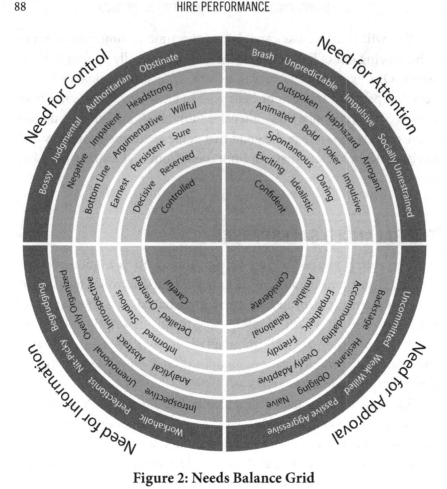

Figure 2: Needs Balance Grid

CONCLUSION

In this chapter, we identified four emotional needs that are universal (everybody's got 'em), innate (you're born with 'em), and intuitive (they occur without thinking). Our research over nearly two decades uncovers five emotional needs that are active in most business conversations. These are:

1. The need for stability—This need is so foundational to the individual's productivity that it belongs at Level 1.
2. The need for attention—When balanced, it helps salespeople

quickly establish rapport; when unbalanced, salespeople talk more than listen and become impatient quickly with details.

3. The need for approval—When balanced, it helps salespeople connect with their customers and prospects with accurate empathy; when unbalanced, it creates in salespeople the fear of rejection and a difficulty with closing sales.

4. The need for information—When balanced, it helps salespeople plan and solve problems; when unbalanced, it leads to an obsessive gathering of data that can slow down the sales process.

5. The need for control—When balanced, it enables salespeople to drive the sales process to a decision; when unbalanced, it can make reps oppositional, refusing to accept change or to be coached.

Top performers possess all four emotional needs in a state of balanced equilibrium. Too much or too little of each can undermine productivity in predictable and painful ways.

10

TEAMWORK ISN'T ACCIDENTAL

Level 3 is not only about individual sales productivity. More care is being taken today than ever before to look at the impact of a hire upon the balance and cohesiveness of the sales team. You may recruit top-notch talent, but put those potential superstars in the wrong sales organization with the wrong manager or the wrong kind of peer mentoring and they may easily fail. In addition to providing a model for understanding individual behavior, the four emotional needs also help you evaluate the impact of the new hire on your existing team. The styles that drive your salespeople to behave with customers in certain predictable ways also shape their approach to team interactions.

TEAMWORK IN THE SALES ENVIRONMENT

Teamwork is a frequently overlooked aspect of selling. Indeed, the American cultural stereotype of a salesperson is that of the competitive, solitary road warrior. Most people perceive selling to be essentially an act of one-on-one persuasion. Words and phrases like "self-starter" and "able to work unsupervised" appear in many sales-recruitment ads. About one-third of sales reps say they were attracted to a sales career because they could control their own time and not have to depend on the performance of others (think controller). Sales organizations exploit individual competitiveness with contests and other incentives to provide momentary productivity boosts. While contests may motivate some to a temporary burst of productivity, they can discourage performance in many other salespeople. For example, analyzers will carefully weigh the odds of winning with the value of the prize and may or may not participate. Empathizers use contests to build relationships with others in the organization. I've seen these strongly approval-oriented reps give away leads to front-runners and become cheerleaders for other salespeople just to improve their popularity. Empathizers care more about cooperating than winning.

Teamwork performs five critical functions in the sales organization.

1. Success modeling

Where do new recruits learn how to succeed or fail in their new job? Not from company-sponsored new-employee orientation classes, that's for sure. Listen to this first-year rep from a tech-services firm. "First thing the guys in the cubicle next to me said after I returned from home office training was 'Forget all the stuff they taught you. We'll tell you how to really do the job right.'"

New recruits watch and talk with veterans in the organization to learn the informal norms, acceptable shortcuts, and performance standards. The team sanctions and perpetuates the real measures of success in the organization.

2. Personal support

Where do reps having trouble go first for counsel, motivation, and mentoring? Not to the manager who just hired them and who they may still feel a need to impress. When salespeople don't know what to do, their first line of support is to confide in each other. Struggling new hires ask trusted peers. The team, more than management, are the first responders to productivity problems. Salespeople compare their activity to others on the team to evaluate how they are really doing, because performance is shaped more by team expectations than decrees from the home office.

3. **Management relationships**

Even if a sales rep works alone in a territory, one's attitude and assumptions about teamwork influence the kind of relationship the new hire builds with his or her manager. That's why great managers build strong teams. When managers trust their teams and roll up their sleeves to work with them on the daily grind of improving productivity, they inspire loyalty and motivate performance. Word gets around the team pretty fast if the manager is a good mentor and coach of sales talent and not merely a bureaucratic babysitter. Effective coaching assumes that both salesperson and manager value teamwork.

4. **Strategic selling**

Big-ticket sales, which can take months, if not a year or more, to close, demand teamwork within the sales organization. A team from the firm must partner with multiple decision makers of the customer. Teamwork skills are also critical for the strategic salesperson to find and nurture the "internal champions" in the prospect company required to move a sale through the often complex maze of bureaucratic hurdles. Consultative selling requires getting on the customer's team.

5. **Customer service**

Attitudes toward teamwork in salespeople contribute to the value they place on customer service. "Lone Ranger" reps seldom follow up the sale with service. Handling complaints, asking for referrals, digging for incremental sales—these activities correlate highly with one's ability to function on a team.

USING EMOTIONAL NEEDS TO PREDICT TEAMWORK

If you are going to recruit a winning team, it's important that you know that teamwork isn't accidental. Success as a team is the same as for the individual. The best teams are those made up of people with balanced behavioral styles.

The graphic in figure 3 will help you better understand the relationship between emotional needs and the behavioral styles they generate. Balance is described by the behaviors within the inner circles.

Let's use the need for control as an example (upper left quadrant). The rep with a balanced need for control is controlled and persistent—admirable traits in a salesperson. As the need for control becomes more unbalanced, the rep becomes assertive, dominant, and perhaps even forceful and intimidating.

Each emotional need in the quadrant acts in a similar way. When behaviors are closer to a balanced state (in the center of the graph), the individual is more likely to be productive. The further from the center, the more influence exerted by that emotional need to undermine productivity.

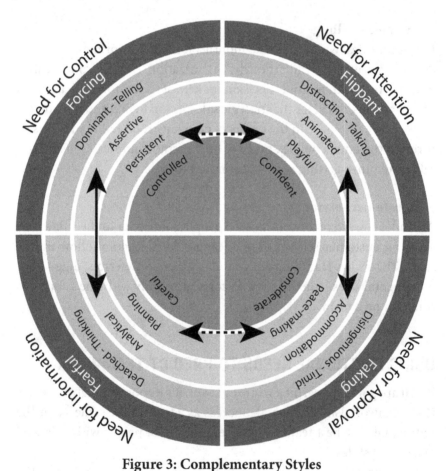

Figure 3: Complementary Styles

COMPATIBLE STYLES BUILD WINNING TEAMS

Some selling styles complement each other. They are synergistic. The strengths of one compensate for weaknesses in the other. When you put these compatible styles together, your sales team is strengthened by maximizing teamwork.

Using the balance grid, the styles adjacent to each other are compatible. We've drawn arrows connecting the compatible styles. Let's look at these in closer detail.

CONTROLLERS AND ANALYZERS

John is very analytical. He never makes snap decisions because he likes to take his time and study all available options. Decisions are often difficult for John when one option isn't the clear choice. When John gets stuck he relies on Kayla. Kayla doesn't seem to agonize over decisions like he does. She may ask one or two bottom-line questions, but then she decides the matter. John admires Kayla because she has an uncanny ability to know what's important and make worry-free decisions. And once that decision is made Kayla doesn't agonize over it. It's done and over with and she's on to the next opportunity.

Kayla operates out of a strong need for control, which over time has developed into the habits and instincts of the controller—someone comfortable with making decisions. Controllers and analyzers are highly compatible. Their styles, though different, work well together. Controllers like to make decisions but are often impatient with gathering details. Analyzers like to work on the fact-finding and agonize over decisions. The strengths of one compensate for the weaknesses of the other. Controllers and analyzers are synergistic. We represent that strong compatibility with a solid arrow in the diagram.

PERFORMERS AND EMPATHIZERS

Elsa is a flashy, loud-talking sales rep who insists on being the life of the party. She tells off-color stories and teases her coworkers. Trevor envies Elsa's outgoing style, but he is also concerned about how others might feel about Elsa's flamboyant ways. He laughs at her jokes, because if he doesn't, Elsa is likely to mock him as a party pooper in front of the rest of the team, and he couldn't endure that. Trevor knows all the office gossip. He's learned that the boss is deeply religious, which makes him annoyed at Elsa's coarse language. Trevor quietly takes Elsa aside at the sales meeting to relate what he's heard. "I don't want you to think I have a problem with it," he tells her, "but I thought you should know."

Elsa's boisterous behavior is typical of performers. The need for attention drives them to be noticed. If there isn't a crowd around, they'll make one. Trevor's behaviors are those of the empathizer style. He is relationally sensitive and very conflict avoidant. Performers and empathizers are complementary styles. Performers need an appreciative audience, someone to laugh at their jokes and admire them (or at least pretend to). Empathizers, on the other hand, need the performer's glibness. Performers find it difficult to come to a conclusion for fear of offending others. They enjoy hanging out with the talkative, spontaneous performers who leave no doubt as to their thoughts and feelings. Empathizer customers like the outgoing amiability of the performer sales reps.

CONTROLLERS AND PERFORMERS

These two styles can work together on a team, but their synergism is less productive than the previous pairs. Perhaps we should say they tolerate each other. We express this less than ideal compatibility with the dotted arrows in the graphic.

Kayla the controller has an idea about implementing a new policy, but she's not sure how others on her team will receive it. She doesn't want to be viewed as uncertain or hesitant in front of the other salespeople, so she calls on Elsa the performer. During their conversation, Kayla skillfully maneuvers the conversation so that Elsa thinks she has actually come up with the new idea. Kayla acts supportive and strokes Elsa's huge ego. Impulsive and attention-driven, Elsa begins to chat up the idea with almost everyone. Kayla watches and waits. If the idea bombs with others in the organization, Elsa catches the flak. If the idea is accepted, Kayla will allow Elsa to take some of the credit, but she'll play on the performer's natural aversion to responsibility and assume full control of the project.

Controllers use the weaknesses of performers. As in the example, controllers may take advantage of the impulsiveness of performers to float trial balloons in the organization or to try risky, unproven ideas. Performers aren't usually threatened by the control needs of the controller, as long as the person in charge exercises minimum accountability and provides opportunities for recognition.

EMPATHIZERS AND ANALYZERS
This is another example of complementary team styles that get along more by default than design. They are compatible but usually don't spur each other on to greater productivity. Both are introverts, content to work unnoticed in the background. Empathizers rarely voice negative opinions, and analyzers mostly keep to themselves. However, it's not uncommon for empathizers to team up with analyzers if they have to confront controllers who have become dictatorial or performers who have grown erratic and unpredictable. Empathizers and analyzers both require an orderly, predictable work environment. They are experts at working behind the scenes to build alliances and manage the flow of information (both factual and political).

CONTRADICTORY STYLES UNDERMINE TEAMWORK

Some styles simply don't get along. Figure 4 shows the styles that can come to cross purposes. They share nothing in common, do not understand each other, and intuitively distrust each other. People with contradictory styles are convinced that the other side is intentionally frustrating them. Put these styles together and invariably you generate conflict, mistrust, and miscommunication on your team.

Some of the styles are like oil and water, or perhaps we could say, like gasoline and fire: they don't mix well. As the solid arrows indicate, they quickly come to cross purposes.

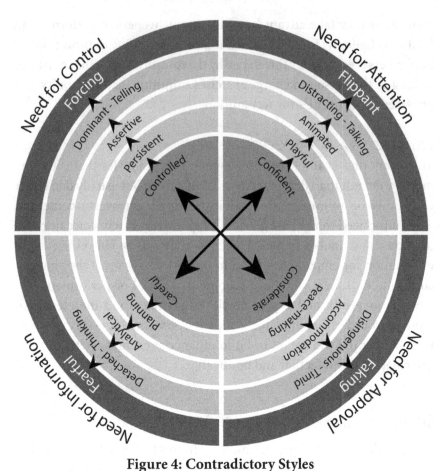

Figure 4: Contradictory Styles

CONTROLLERS AND EMPATHIZERS

A powerful invisible wedge separates controllers and empathizers. Controllers talk about empathizers as bleeding hearts. Empathizers describe controllers as coldhearted and insensitive. Each accuses the other of having serious character flaws.

Their emotional needs are completely at odds with each other. As extroverted, task-oriented individuals, controllers seldom care about the personal feelings of others that are so critical to the empathizer. Controllers are bottom-line decision makers. Empathizers are introverted and people oriented. That strong approval need makes them sensitive to criticism. Empathizers are not competitive, like controllers, but value cooperation and teamwork. Controllers and empathizers are complete opposites. Without the mediating influence of a performer to reduce the tension with a joke or an analyzer to speak unemotionally (compatible styles to their own), they don't communicate well and they probably distrust each other.

PERFORMERS AND ANALYZERS

Performers and analyzers get cross-wise with each other a lot. The more out of balance the attention and approval emotional needs, the more these teammates frustrate each other. Performers are extroverted and playful, while analyzers tend to be introverted and serious. Performers may publicly ridicule analyzers, calling them anal-retentive (the term has great shock value). Analyzers are convinced that performers are shallow and phony and may collect information on bad business practice to show to the boss. Their styles clash because each needs exactly the emotional resource in which the other is most deficient.

IDENTICAL EXTROVERTED STYLES

Controllers don't do well in their initial meetings with other strongly control-oriented people. Their strong competitive nature and territorialism make the possibilities for teamwork similar to that of two male lions within close proximity of each other. They instinctively become combative. There can usually be only one true controller on any team. If there are two, they frequently resort to Machiavellian power plays until one is forced to retreat. However, once the alpha-controller is established, the other control-oriented team member may settle in and become productive as long as the alpha-controller leaves him or her in peace. Controllers need to know who is in charge, and once that's firmly established they often appear to adjust and work well.

The other extroverted pairing that frequently undermines productivity is performer with performer. Picture two actors hamming it up on the stage, each trying to upstage the other. Put two performers too close together and you could have chaos as each tries to outdo the other, distracting anyone within earshot.

If you want to get a better understanding of the concept of contradictory behaviors, tune in to the latest reality TV show. Why are these programs so popular? Yes, they get ratings. Why? Because it's fun to watch people fighting and doing stupid things to undermine each other and sometimes to help each other. It's all about contradictory emotionally unbalanced participants. They fight, they complain about each other behind each other's backs, they do stupid things, they cry on a dime; now that's fun to watch. If you have all your emotional needs in balance you'll never get on reality TV. Think of these programs as a real-life laboratory for style incompatibility.

DOUBLE TROUBLE

Human behavior is very complex. Barnett developed the integrated model from real-time sales research to help managers explain human behavior and teamwork variables. So far in this book, we've talked about controllers and empathizers and analyzers and performers, but people are seldom, if ever, one pure style. Since everybody possesses all these emotional needs in varying proportions, most people are combinations of styles. In fact, salespeople can be comfortable in one style of behavior on the job and behave in a completely different way at home. Their emotional needs may vary with the many roles we all must play with the important people in our lives.

In this chapter, you've learned that individual styles contradict or complement each other on a team. The assumption has been that styles were embodied in different individuals. But some people carry around conflicting styles within themselves. They are a walking contradiction of emotional needs. They want control *and* approval, attention *and* information. People possessed by contradictory out-of-balance emotional needs are the most difficult people to manage because they find it so difficult to manage themselves.

Unbalanced contradictory styles within an individual create two conditions, both of which have severe repercussions both for personal productivity and for effective teamwork: conflicted reps and double-down reps. These conditions are admittedly difficult to spot with the naked eye. They are more easily diagnosed using the SalesKey profile, designed specifically to detect and measure the relative strength of salespeople's emotional needs. But you should know that these emotional needs can become quite complex and for the sake of completeness must be documented.

CONFLICTED REPS

Each style has its opposite. Those are the incompatible needs addressed above. There are two types of conflicted reps: the performer-analyzer and the controller-empathizer.

PERFORMER-ANALYZER: THE TEAM INNOVATOR

Based on our studies of nearly ten thousand salespeople, the more common conflicted rep pattern is that of the performer-analyzer. The inner clash of incompatible emotional needs arises from the extroverted, impulsive style of the performer at odds with the introverted, detail-oriented analyzer pattern. In a recent study of 942 salespeople from different companies and different industries, we discovered a significant correlation between scores of performer-analyzers and high creativity scores. This confirms what we've been saying for some time: performer-analyzers like to play the role of the team innovator. The analyzer side studies and creates new ways to approach tasks and innovative solutions to problems. The performer behavior fuels the chutzpah to go out on a limb and share their ideas with others. They like to promote what they've discovered. Teams usually benefit from team innovators. However, some performer-analyzers can become unbalanced in their emotional intensity; their love of innovation undermines productivity with excessive experimentation.

For example, Ted is always thinking up new approaches to customers. He continually experiments with his conversation starters to see how to make his engagement statement more effective. Finding one, Ted uses it for a while and then abandons it as soon as he thinks of a new way to refine his presentation. Ted's manager wonders why Ted won't use the company's standard presentation materials. But Ted would rather spend hours designing new computer slide shows with animation and built-in programming than actually use the presentation to make sales. If Ted's manager ignores Ted's ideas, Ted becomes resentful and threatens to quit and go to work for someone who will listen to his ideas. What Ted actually does is to start designing still another new system.

Ted is a team innovator, using his analytical skills to drive his attention needs. He thrives on the recognition he expects for building that better mousetrap. Innovators on sales teams are difficult to manage, because selling is based on repetition, doing the same things repeatedly with new prospects. Repetition is extremely difficult for performer-analyzers who change things constantly to "improve" them.

EMPATHIZER-CONTROLLER: THE TEAM POLITICO

The second type of conflicted rep is the empathizer-controller. This is the rarest behavioral style among salespeople, showing up in less than 5 percent of the population we've so far tested. We describe the empathizer-controller as the team politico. An exaggerated emotional need for control need collides with the need to be universally loved and appreciated to create a behavioral style that uses people skills to amass and maintain control.

Carlos is an example of this type of conflicted rep. He can't walk into a meeting without becoming instantly aware of the social dynamics at work in the room. He has a knack for knowing what people are thinking and feeling just by watching them. He has learned to use this sixth sense to his advantage. He not only senses the emotional climate but can quickly analyze the power climate of the room as well; who is really in control and who are the followers. Carlos gets what he wants by playing people off against each other. He manipulates. One of his close friends on the sales team jokingly refers to him as Machiavelli—the fifteenth-century author of *The Prince*, a how-to book for control freaks. Carlos is never belligerent or forceful. He's a smooth operator. He makes things happen by subtle manipulation and convincing everyone that he is only looking out for their best interest. For example, Carlos is scheduled for a private, confidential meeting next week with the regional VP to discuss some concerns he has with his current district manager, who knows nothing about the meeting.

Think of politicians—people who are comfortable with power but do not threaten others with their ambition. They have a knack for telling people what they want to hear. These are the signature behaviors of the empathizer-controller. Politicos hardly ever show up on the radar as problem producers. They are experts at staying out of trouble, working the system to their advantage. The first time many managers even notice a problem is when they discover that the team politico has created a mutiny among the field force and manipulated a naïve manager into a career-ending corner.

Not everyone with strong emotional needs for control and approval wants to take over the team, but that is clearly one agenda for the serious politico. His ambition is to grab his boss's job through passive-aggressiveness and killing with kindness. Once he becomes manager, he sets his sights on positions higher in the organization. Team politicos are productive only as long as their output serves to move them up and along the chain of command. Selling is clearly secondary to managerial ambition. They excel at building strong sales teams. They are seldom impulsive, always highly self-controlled, competitive, goal driven, and able to build rapport and loyalty with their reps.

THE DOUBLE-DOWNS

What about the person with an unbalanced strong emotional need and a strongly avoidant pattern (unbalanced on the low end) in its contradictory quadrant? We refer to this situation as a push, and it creates a classification of team members who are very entrenched in their ways. They are called double-downs because this combination of contradictory needs has the effect of doubling the negative impact of the out-of-balance style. The strong negative avoidance of one need pushes its corresponding opposite need even higher.

You are not likely to diagnose this condition without a SalesKey Level 3 analysis. Without the assessment tool, you are likely to see double-down as merely a very strong style. SalesKey and its ability to differentiate the motivations of salespeople down to such a fine resolution is extremely helpful in pinpointing the communication effectiveness or deficiency a candidate may bring to a team.

As an example, Jason's SalesKey profile shows an extremely high attention need score. He also has a very, very low information need. Both emotional needs are unbalanced, one high and one low. In Jason's case, the conflicts inherent in these two contradictory styles synergize, but not in the direction of productivity. We know that performers are impulsive and tend to rely more on intuition than facts for decision making. His low analyzer score doubles the impact of these unproductive behaviors. The low analyzer style means that Jason not only craves attention but that he avoids analysis. If Jason's analyzer need were more balanced, it would offset some of the detail avoidance common to all performers. We call this a pull. But Jason's low analyzing is a push to his emotional need for attention. The contradictory styles reinforce the negative behaviors of each.

The push could go the other way; that is, a high analyzer and a low attention, like the profile belonging to Alex, for example. He's a double-down analyzer, more comfortable with computers than people. He is excessively task oriented and holds on to every piece of paper that crosses his desk. Alex has more file cabinets that anyone else in the firm. His low performer pushes his analyzer over the top.

Let's move to the empathizer-controller pair. Bill is both a strong empathizer and at the same time control avoidant. This doubles the potency of his empathizer style. Most salespeople have a control need strong enough to tell them when it's time to stop visiting and start closing the sale. Not Bill. His productivity suffers from a terribly costly push.

THE OPPOSITIONAL

Jack's push is the most destructive of all styles, however. A strong control need coexisting with approval avoidance creates the oppositional pattern. You must be able to spot oppositionals if you are going to recruit a winning sales team. If you get one of these folks on your sales force, it could take you months to undo the damage. Here's the distinguishing feature: like anyone with a strong emotional need for control, they don't want anyone telling them what to do. But the oppositional adds that low approval push; they don't care what others on the team think about them. They like to provoke conflict. They are called oppositionals because they are likely to do the exact opposite of what they are told or what is expected. They mean to assert their independence, and they don't care who gets in the way.

Jack arrives late and leaves early from most meetings he attends. If the expectation is to be on time and participatory, Jack does the opposite. He dresses up on casual day and wears khakis when everyone else is in a suit. Jack loves to say no. Although very effective with some types of customers, he drives his manager crazy. Jack is openly critical, often hostile, and refuses to be coached, advised, or managed. His conflicted needs for high control and low approval make Jack uncooperative. Oppositionals are not team players, and they will tell you so. Most controllers have a strong enough approval need to value teamwork and get along with others. Their balanced emotional need for acceptance pulls the control need back a little more into balance. Oppositionals not only do not need the approval of others but behave in ways that repel it. They are Lone Rangers who undermine teamwork.

PREDICTING FIT

By spending some time understanding these concepts, you can begin to predict exactly what behaviors you are likely to see when you bring a candidate on board or recommend an applicant to a team leader. Level 3 empowers you to understand whether a candidate represents a good fit for your company's culture and the team on which he will be required to function. If teamwork is important in your organization, hiring an oppositional (high control, low approval) rep is not going to have a positive outcome. If you need someone to work alone in a territory with minimal accountability to a team, the lone-wolf behavior becomes less of a concern. If you are the manager, you can begin to work with the oppositional to understand how his or her emotional needs may alienate some types of buyers. By knowing how the new hire is likely to fit into the team, you can improve the chances that the salesperson will hit his or her potential. Understanding teamwork and style compatibility is absolutely critical to keeping your turnover rates down.

CONCLUSION

Hire Performance demands an understanding of teamwork. In this chapter we discussed how people often have more than one unbalanced emotional need. Four need combinations are compatible and may synergize in higher productivity:

1. Controllers and analyzers are the most compatible, as decision makers and fact gatherers collaborate.
2. Performers and empathizers synergize each other's social skills.
3. Analyzers and empathizers are both introverted types; they get along well on a team, although indecision may reign if there's no controller around.
4. Controllers use performers to test out ideas without taking flack.

Other need combinations whether in groups or within an individual are incompatible. These pairings should be avoided.

1. Analyzers and performers typically don't work well together on a team, although some individuals with this pattern may be team innovators.
2. Controllers and empathizers will never understand each other.
3. Conflicted reps are those with two strong incompatible needs.
4. The double-downs are salespeople with strong drives in one need and also in its opposite need. The effect is to double the negative impact.

Sales organizations, like individuals, are more productive when they are made up of a balance of behavioral styles. Productivity is enhanced when compatible styles synergize and reps with conflicting styles are weeded out.

11

LEVEL 4: EXCEEDING EXPECTATIONS

So far we've explored Levels 1, 2, and 3 of the Four Levels of Sales model, which helps recruiters identify and prioritize what to look for in sales candidates. The first three levels are the expectations of anyone who wants to be in sales. Level 4 behaviors are those skills and aptitudes required by a specific company if a rep is going to exceed the expectations of being good enough to become a sales superstar. Level 4 is about learning to work smarter when you can't work any harder (Level 1—effort), any more efficiently (Level 2), or any more effectively (Level 3). Most of the time, recruiters will not need to worry about Level 4. It's usually enough to match a candidate to a position three levels deep. But sometimes recruiters will need to delve into some Level 4 recruiting.

The most frequent type of Level 4 evaluation you will need to do as a sales recruiter involves the types of contact approaches used by the firm. How are salespeople expected to contact clients and prospects? If these aren't spelled out specifically in the job description, you will need to know this information.

Two obvious Level 4 behaviors fall into this category that you will probably need to explore in most if not all applicants:

- using the telephone
- asking for referrals

PHONE PRESENCE

People develop quirks about using the telephone. Either they don't want to be rudely treated as a telemarketer when they call or they need visual feedback when talking to someone. Empathizers and performers shy away from the phone because they can't see the visual clues that are so important to them. The empathizer can't see if the person is happy or upset; the performer can't tell whether he has the customer's undivided attention or not. Checking for emotional blocks to using the phone will be more important if the candidate is expected to call consumers at their homes. Businesses are usually better prepared to handle the unexpected sales call than people at home are. Do-not-call lists, the proliferation of mobile phones, and various phone-screening technologies have all but made telephone cold calling obsolete.

Determining your applicant's comfort on the phone may be a little more difficult than you might imagine. That's because anyone can pick up the phone and make a call without much hesitation. The issue with using the phone in most sales jobs is the repetition, day in and day out dialing fifty to a hundred times and then waiting to hear the reaction to your call from someone you have obviously interrupted. In most cases, people we interrupt by calling on them on the phone begin that conversation in the controller mode. They don't know you, and even if they do, chances aren't good that they want to talk at that very moment unless you're returning their call. The only thing on the interrupted person's mind is how to politely (and sometimes not so politely) get rid of you so they can get back to what they were doing. This kind of one-sided insensitivity is purely controller-like. Unfortunately, how do most businesses train their salespeople to behave on that call? Like empathizers—sweet, unobtrusive, deflecting expected anger with such lies as "I'm not selling anything" or "We're taking a survey" (really?). If lying about the purpose of your call doesn't develop emotional barriers to phone use, you only need to remember what we learned about the compatibility of the empathizer style with that of controllers. They aren't compatible at all. They are completely contradictory styles. No wonder a lot of salespeople have developed a kind of telephobia. They've been poorly trained to fail.

Once you are satisfied that your candidate meets most of the criteria set up in the first three levels, and if using the telephone is critical to the position, here are three ways to assess the applicant's Level 4 phone presence.

1. **Ask about phone usage at their previous job.**
   Obviously, you want to know how your candidate used the phone in previous sales jobs. You should inquire into the kind of training, if any, they may have received. Ask about the methods used to initiate calls. Did they have to tell half-truths or lies? Also inquire as to how much time they spent on the phone each day. Were they required to make a certain number of phone contacts? How does this experience compare to the position you are offering?

   In addition to what the person says, pay attention to how he or she is saying it. Look for shifts in body posture, a change in the energy of one's self-presentation, or other nonverbal clues that might indicate an emotional hesitation to use the phone.

2. **Require the candidate to leave a phone message.**
   One recruiter we know who works at a phone center where people are on the phone all day long requires candidates to call a toll-free number and leave a five-minute voice-mail message. He tells them a little about the position; that it requires talking on the phone a lot every day. Then he asks them to introduce themselves and tell why they think they should be considered for the job. Of course, he gathers much valuable intelligence on applicants by doing this. Not only does he hear the clarity of their voice and their ability to speak professionally, but he listens for the emotional tone of their voice. Are they nervous (high risk sensitivity)? Are they soft-spoken and understated (empathizers)? Are they matter-of-fact and a little pushy (controllers)? Are they over-the-top loud and exuberant and can't finish the message in less than five minutes (performers)? Do they speak in a bit of a monotone and emphasize facts (analyzers)?

The biggest benefit of this technique is that people who don't
have initiative and have problems with the phone self-select out
of the process and never leave a message.

3. **Ask the candidate to make a phone call as you observe.**
   This is an optional follow-up if the phone message described
   above still leaves some doubt in your mind as to the phone
   presence of the candidate. This would probably be best done in
   a second or even third interview, not right out of the gate. If the
   person is currently a phone rep, ask her to call an associate (who
   is prepared for the call) and give her standard phone opening.
   You may want to coach the associate, depending on how difficult
   or easy you want to make the experience. If your applicant has
   no appropriate experience, give him a printed script of your
   phone dialogue model and let him study it and ask questions
   about it.

   In either case you will learn valuable information, such as what
   the veteran is used to doing to get decision makers on the phone
   or how the newbie approaches the task you've assigned. Does
   the inexperienced person ask the right kind of questions about
   the script? Does the overconfident applicant just read it over and
   begin the call?

   During the call, watch and listen. Where does her energy go
   during this exercise? Is she standing and pacing? Does she throw
   a pencil in the air or take copious notes? These energy leaks
   could indicate that the rep is coping with stress of the task rather
   than focusing on the task itself. Look at the person's face. Is it
   relaxed and smiling? Is it stressed and serious? You are looking
   for signs of emotional discomfort that could indicate that a daily
   regimen of phone calling could lead to early burnout. Where do
   the eyes go? Are they focused or looking around in an attempt
   to find something interesting to engage their attention?

   One word of caution: it's possible that individuals who suffer from stage fright may become a little unhinged performing in front of you. One way to handle this is to use a video camera to record the applicant's call and then debrief it later. But there is some evidence in our research that people who suffer from performance anxiety may not perform well in a phone center if they know they can be overheard by others. Our advice is to hire only those who are able to make the call in a more relaxed state, who focus on the conversation and ask questions with a smile in their voice.

ASKING FOR REFERRALS

Given the difficulty of cold calling in today's marketplace, the professional salesperson needs to make as many warm calls as possible. The most readily available source of leads should come from the current customer base of satisfied buyers. Most sales organizations rely on salespeople generating leads from referrals, but very seldom is this skill included in the requirements for a sales position. Many recruiters may think that it's a simple thing to ask for a referral and every salesperson probably does it. Well, the truth is that in a recent study of 1,358 salespeople, we found that 38 percent of them indicate that they have some difficulty asking current customers for referrals. Fourteen percent simply don't ask although they have been trained in how to. People can ask, but the fact is that they don't ask.

There are several key reasons why salespeople shy away from asking current customers and prospects for the names of friends, family, and business associates. Empathizers fear appearing pushy or rude to their current clients. People with an out-of-balance approval need don't like to put people in any position where they might say no. Analyzers justify not asking for referrals by their fear that it might jeopardize the current sale. The other major cause of poor referral generation is that companies discourage their reps from doing it, usually a result of a referral-reluctant VP of sales who may have had a bad experience or two asking for a referral, institutionalizing his own poor productivity.

If your firm expects its salespeople to generate warm leads by asking for referrals, you should probably evaluate this Level 4 behavior. Here are two ways:

1. **Ask experienced reps about referrals at the previous job.**
   Did the company they worked for expect salespeople to get referrals? If not, why did they avoid this source of warm leads? Are these excuses likely to carry over into the new job with this candidate? If they did expect salespeople to generate referrals, ask your applicant to describe the method he or she used. Can the candidate remember the approach? If not, chances are that wasn't part of his or her selling. If the applicant can remember the referral question, is it effective? Will the salesperson need to be retrained? Finally, ask how many referrals a week or a month the sales veteran generated in his last job. Does he answer with a number or does the answer contain some excuse?

2. **Ask the applicant to give you a referral to someone who might be looking for a better sales job.**
   Okay, do you the recruiter have a way of asking for referrals, or do you leave this avenue of lead generation alone? We know of several cases where a recruiter asked a candidate about whom else she knew who might like to work for the firm. In one case, the candidate readily came up with several names of sales reps working at another firm. When the recruiter followed up on the referred leads, two of the individuals eventually came to work for the firm and became top performers.

   What does it mean if your applicant says he or she doesn't know anyone to refer or just defers on giving a referral? Now obviously, if you are recruiting a narrow segment of the population to a highly skilled position, it's certainly reasonable that someone might not know others with the same experience or training. But if this job is fairly standard and your candidate says she doesn't know other salespeople or comes up with some other excuse for not naming someone, you may be dealing with a hesitation to work her personal sphere of influence. Chances are very good that if a person doesn't like to give referrals, that individual is not going to ask people for referrals.

LEVERAGING COMPANY-SPECIFIC REQUIREMENTS

Besides the kinds of contacts the firm uses, recruiters may need to evaluate other Level 4 behaviors specific and perhaps unique to a company. These include two broad categories:

1. Leveraging specific nonsales experience
2. Changing corporate sales culture

Some recruiters will be asked to look for knowledge and skills that are not related to selling but to the product or service being sold. The more technical the product or service, the more the sales recruiter may need to evaluate the degree of proficiency in specific skill sets. These Level 4 behaviors could be anything from fields of study to experience with certain software programs. Evaluating these characteristics is usually pretty straightforward. You can simply ask about the applicant's training or knowledge in those specific fields.

It's a little more difficult when the company is trying to change its sales culture; that is, how they sell, whom they sell to, and what they sell. We have a manufacturer as a client. Caught in the squeeze of commodity pricing, they decided to differentiate themselves from the competition by recruiting and training salespeople to move from a transactional focus on price and availability to a more strategic sale focused on delivering value. Reps were trained to interact at a higher level of expertise with the clients, asking them questions about business efficiencies. Instead of just taking orders and quoting bulk discounts, salespeople were expected to consult with customers about best practices in all phases of their business. The company wanted to recruit people who could do all that was expected of a manufacturer's rep, but they also wanted to see some behaviors that they knew from their experience would help that rep exceed expectations and add value to the business relationship. The VP of training asked us if we could add some questions to SalesKey that would help them measure what they called "business aptitude." We said that we would gladly do it and included the items they had worked out were critical for someone to succeed at this new sales strategy in their industry.

Your company may be looking at a specific change that they are hoping to implement. You will need to ask the hiring authorities about the behaviors they are looking for and add those to your interview process of applicants. This will help the new hire not only fit in but exceed expectations.

CONCLUSION

Level 4 recruiting focuses on those behaviors that are specific and sometimes unique to the situation of the company. The most common Level 4 behaviors are those that are used by the firm to initiate contacts with prospects and current customers. We looked at two of these that are usually important to almost any sales position.

1. Phone presence—We shared several techniques for evaluating the applicant's comfort using the telephone. Any hesitation to smile and dial can drain energy and contribute to burnout.
2. Asking for referrals—Many good salespeople never attain the peak productivity of Level 4 because they are hesitant to ask current customers and prospects to help them develop leads.

We also identified Level 4 behaviors as those specific skills, experience, and knowledge a salesperson might require working in a specific field or those deemed critical for an anticipated change in the company's sales culture.

12

LEVERAGING THE PAY PLAN

Note: This rest of this book is going to address specific Level 4 skills and aptitudes necessary for you, the sales recruiter, to exceed the expectations of the hiring authorities for whom you work. These skills add to the foundational selling skills of Levels 1, 2, and 3 and position you to do a better job in the specific marketplace in which you compete. Not all of these Level 4 skills will fit every recruiter, but the information may be helpful should you need to modify your approach or marketing strategy.

You've thought through a strategic planning process necessary for Hire Performance. You've looked at your hiring philosophy and may have begun to confront your own recruitment reluctance. You know the Four Levels of Selling, which contain the key objective criteria for sales success, and you've been introduced to an integrated model for understanding both individual and team productivity. But there's still one more skill you must address before you're ready to advertise for candidates. What does your pay plan say about the kind of salespeople you can or should recruit? If you're the entrepreneur putting together a compensation plan, which one should you use?

QUESTIONS FOR DETERMINING A PAY PLAN

Here are some questions that can help you think through a winning pay plan for your sales team.

Is the sales cycle long or short?

The sales cycle is the amount of time it takes a rep to move from prospecting to closing a sale. If you sell a big-ticket item, the sales cycle may last months or even a year or more as in strategic sales. The longer it takes to go through all the steps necessary to clinch the deal, the less you should rely on a commission-only pay plan. Not many salespeople can or will wait months between paychecks. Selling that takes months for "inside champions" to move the sale through many decision-making levels require pay plans that maximize the base pay and reward outstanding production with bonuses or incentives. Commission sales work best with short sales cycles and products for which nearly everyone may be a prospect.

How difficult will it be to find a candidate with the necessary skills, education, or experience to do the job?

The more difficult the position is to fill, the less you should rely on a commission-only comp plan. Qualifications translate into guaranteed income for salespeople. High commissions work best for entry-level, unskilled sales positions. But remember: commission-only selling almost guarantees very high rates of churn. While some personalities may be inspired by the opportunity of "unlimited income," money may not always be the strongest motivator for mature, long-term business relationships.

How long does it take the candidate to finish training and build a customer base?

Sales organizations today spend more than ever on training. Extensive product lines require additional instruction. More and more twenty-first-century jobs depend on complex technology. It is not unusual for reps to need training in computer-based reporting-and-relationship-management programs (CRMs), Internet or intranet systems, sophisticated telecommunications options, and more. It is unreasonable to expect the salesperson to shoulder the financial responsibility of learning the ropes. Longer ramp-up time means you'll probably need to invest more in base pay at start-up and then gradually shift to commissions as the candidate gains skills and becomes more self-sustaining.

What's the going rate? What is the most common pay plan for the position in your industry?
You don't have to phone your competitor to discover how they pay their reps. You can get a clear picture relatively quickly by looking at job placement ads, checking out the salary requirements on résumés, and discussing the candidates' previous compensation packages. Other resources for determining pay plans include your local chamber of commerce, trade publications surveys, government agencies (such as the US Bureau of Labor Statistics), and job-related Internet sites, many of which feature salary range finders that tell you exactly what high-, average-, and low-paying positions pay for a whole range of occupations in your city.

SALARY, COMMISSION, OR DRAW?

Your compensation package telegraphs two strategic pieces of information about you and your business to prospective candidates:

- how important you consider the position to be
- how much turnover you're willing to accept

In most of the world, salaried sales positions are the norm. In the last decade, many sales organizations in the United States have also frowned on commission-only selling. With the advent of customer-oriented sales techniques, sales gurus and trainers have convinced many that commission-only selling represents a conflict of interest. They contend that a rep working on commission will prefer to sell what is good for the salesperson and not necessarily what is good for the customer. These assumptions are often rooted in negative experiences with unethical salespeople that can generate a negative attitude toward selling in general (poor sales identity). Eliminating commission-based selling has lowered turnover in some organizations, but it has come at the price of productivity. Salaried sales jobs tend to attract less-motivated, more risk-avoidant people. Building a new business requires a spirit of entrepreneurship that is born in passion and nurtured by risk.

The most common sales compensation program found today in the United States is a combination of some salary (called a "base") and some incentive referred to as a commission or bonus. This pay plan gives the starting rep the security of some income while giving the salesperson the opportunity to increase his or her income by making more sales than may be required just to keep one's job.

THREE COMMISSION OPTIONS

Here are three ways to work with a commission.

Advance against commission

This option prepays commissions to the salesperson when a sale is made. Advance plans are popular in industries where customers sign long-term payment contracts, such as insurance or security sales. Although the company may not receive full payment of the contract in advance, the company advances all or part of the commission in exchange for the salesperson's agreement to pay back the advance as the contract is fulfilled month by month. In effect, the company creates a credit arrangement with its sales force. This plan requires legal contracts that set limits on the time or the amount of advance a salesperson receives as well as specifying what happens if the salesperson leaves the company or the customer cancels payment on the contract. Advance plans require sophisticated accounting and tracking resources for sales management.

Benefit: Allows salespeople to be paid soon after and during start-up
Liability: Company loses if sales don't match commissions

Guaranteed Draw against Commission

A "draw" pays a salary for a specified time period whether the salesperson makes any sales or not. Commissions are only paid after sales surpass a level determined by the company sufficient to offset the costs of the guaranteed base. The base pay option may continue or be discontinued. The larger the base pay, the lower the commission percentage.

> Benefit: Allows the company to budget sales costs more efficiently
> Liability: Usually involves some salary cap that can demotivate some salespeople

Commission Only

Generally speaking, commission-only jobs are perceived to be more expendable and therefore less attractive to more experienced candidates. Successful sales veterans may prefer the unlimited income opportunity of the commission-only package, but they are a vanishing breed. If you expect reps to underwrite their own start-up costs, you limit your pool of qualified, available candidates significantly. Commission-only pay plans may lower the company's financial risk, but they guarantee higher turnover rates, particularly if you are recruiting candidates for an entry-level position.

This structure usually pays a higher commission rate due to the extra risk absorbed by the salesperson. Without generating sales, the salesperson doesn't get paid. In order for this system to work, your product or service must be able to be sold quickly and frequently to a large client base.

> Benefit: Unlimited income potential for the motivated sales pro
> Liability: Little company loyalty among salespeople; higher turnover

INCENTIVES AND PERQUISITES

Special incentives and perquisites can be an important ingredient in your overall sales-compensation package. Perks are benefits received by an employee in addition to wages and bonuses. Perks include group insurance plans, company car, credit unions, retirement savings plans, and free child care. Perks help offset the disadvantages of any pay plan. For example, to minimize turnover in a commission-only pay plan, you could structure a longevity incentive by linking commission rates to tenure. The longer a salesperson stays with the firm, the higher the commission rate earned on every sale.

Don't confuse perks and incentives. Incentives have value that exceeds their cost. Giving cash is not an incentive but a bonus. The value of cash equals its cost. Incentives are worth more than they usually cost. Allowing the employee of the month to park in a favored parking space costs the company nothing but may be quite valuable if convenient parking is at a premium. Businesses may be able to purchase vacation packages at greatly reduced cost to offer them as prizes for superior sales performance.

Understanding the emotional needs of your top producers gives managers an easy and uncannily accurate framework for structuring incentives. If you know what motivates an individual's behavior, you can devise incentives that satisfy those basic emotional needs. Seen this way, incentives can actually become part of the training-and-development program. They can help salespeople get unbalanced emotional needs back into equilibrium.

Each selling style is motivated by different incentives. For example, empathizers with a high need for approval value time off for social gatherings with friends and coworkers. Performers (high need for attention) jump through hoops for anything they associate with special status, such as trophies or awards they can display prominently in their office or watches or expensive pens they can flash. A tablet computer might thrill the excessively analytical rep but mean nothing to controllers, who can be notoriously antitechnology. Examples of powerful incentives for the controller include a power lunch with the company president or the chance to be on an advisory or policy board.

Don't overlook benefits that may not be quite so obvious, such as proximity of work to where the salesperson lives (less time in traffic), control over one's own time (more freedom), casual dress code (more relaxed atmosphere), or that you provide an office and/or administrative help (less time spent on paperwork).

Think about the incentives as well as the perks of the position. Talk them up in your interview. They are a major selling point as you attempt to recruit top salespeople to your organization and away from your competition.

CONCLUSION

The first Level 4 behavior for you, the recruiter, to leverage is to leverage your pay plan. Many salespeople go into sales so they can earn more money the harder they work. Most sales organizations use some kind of commission structure to reward the productivity of salespeople. Higher guarantees or a generous base salary usually mean lower commission rates. On the other hand, higher commissions mean lower draws or lower base pay. Incentives and perks should be carefully matched to the needs of candidates, as they should be an important part of your compensation package.

13

WHERE TO LOOK FOR
QUALIFIED CANDIDATES

This Level 4 skill applies more to the independent recruiter than to the in-house corporate talent scout. Corporate recruiters that we spoke to get 60 percent of their leads on qualified candidates from their corporate website, only 20 percent from Internet sites, and about 20 percent from referrals. The more technical the job, the more specialized the position, the more likely the firm is to advertise on the online job boards. But let's say you're the sales manager of a small business or the HR person for a new start-up business, and you're ready to start your search for your next top producer. Where will you look for qualified candidates for your sales position? At this point in your recruiting, you're just like the salesperson who has completed product training and is ready to go prospecting. Hire Performance is often won or lost right here, at the starting line. You've analyzed and prepared. Now it's time to meet and greet. And that's prospecting!

If you are weak at trolling for talent, you will recruit salespeople who don't like to prospect either. Your recruitment reluctance will be reflected in their sales reluctance. An old proverb says, "The stream never rises higher than its source." You can't expect to build a winning sales team of contact-initiating, goal-driven salespeople if you yourself can't, won't, or don't know your own success ratios and work them religiously. If you are a manager who must recruit, think of this stage as earning your right to operate a winning sales team.

When it comes to where you look for qualified candidates, we want to recommend that you consider tapping into some free recruiting resources and that you avoid paying for Internet job sites, newspapers, and headhunters.

WHY WE DON'T RECOMMEND INTERNET JOB SITES

When the first edition of this book came out, it was a job-seekers' market. Jobs were plentiful; qualified people were hard to find. Internet job search sites were proliferating but were still relatively new. Today the pendulum has swung back the other way: lean economic times mean it's a recruiter's market with many, many qualified people and few good-paying jobs. Paul Solman of Public Broadcasting says it takes between nine months and two years to find a professional job. This glut of talent has forced the job search engines to create sophisticated programs to weed through millions of applications to match the precise need of employers. No human being reviews résumés anymore. It's all done by machines. Wharton Professor Peter Cappelli says in his book, *Why Good People Can't Get Jobs,* "Job boards are far less effective today than they were in the days when jobs were plentiful. The recruiter writes the ad copy and then inputs some key words. The software takes it from there, deciding who is and who is not qualified. One firm advertised for a standard engineer job and received 29,000 applicants, among whom the software decided that none was qualified."

Here's why we don't like using Internet job boards for your search.

1.　You will be inundated with résumés. Even if you customize your key words carefully, there are so many people looking for work that your e-mail inbox will be swamped. If you had nothing else to do but read résumés, you could never get through a fraction of them. And even then, as in the illustration above, you might not find want you're looking for.

2. Job ads require little if any initiative from the applicant. It takes a few mouse clicks to copy and paste a résumé, choose a firm, and click Apply Now. Your company may have been only one of two hundred that this applicant sent a résumé to just that day. Imagine if ten thousand people did the same thing that particular day and again the next day. It's a shotgun approach that rarely hits anything.

3. The word is getting out that these Internet job sites have become a waste of time if you really need to find a job. They give applicants the impression that they've done something to look for a job. We know from our own experience with these job boards that after submitting nearly nine hundred résumés, we would check the e-mail every waking hour of every day and after more than two years, get nothing in response.

4. The dynamic is all wrong. If you go after someone whose ad appears on an Internet job search site, it puts the applicant in the driver's seat as far as any negotiation is concerned. You want the applicant to find you so they remain in the supplicant position when it comes time to negotiate the employment contract. This is why most major companies recruit primarily through their own company website. Not only is the price less expensive per ad placed, but the inquiry starts with the applicant and not the company.

WHY WE DON'T RECOMMEND NEWSPAPERS

A decade ago when we asked our client companies where they found their sales talent, it was about 15 percent on the Internet and 25 percent by some kind of referral from an employee; the rest were via want ads in newspapers or some other print media. Recently we asked that same question, and none of our large corporate clients use newspapers at all. About 60 percent of new hires come through the company website; about 25 percent still come from personal referrals; and the rest come through some Internet search service. Here's why we recommend that you ignore newspapers.

- Newspapers don't reach young urban professionals. Younger professional job seekers get their information from social media and the Internet. Newspapers try to accommodate this by moving their want ads to an online service (see Why We Don't Recommend Internet Job Sites).
- Newspapers are another shotgun approach to recruiting guaranteed to generate a lot of résumés from nontechnical people for the recruiter to wade through in search of that single pearl.
- Many newspaper ads just refer the reader to the company's website to apply (see Why We Don't Recommend Internet Job Sites).
- Newspaper want ads may work if you are advertising a commission-only or a part-time, nontechnical, entry-level job. It just doesn't seem to be the neighborhood for skilled professionals like it used to be.
- Newspaper ads of the appropriate size can be very expensive and don't improve your chances of finding a quality candidate.

WHY WE DON'T RECOMMEND HEADHUNTERS

Most companies today want to control the selection process and have hired in-house recruiters dedicated to finding sales talent specific to the needs of the business. Here's why we think you should steer clear of fee-based and contingency-based headhunters.

- They are little more than résumé collectors and call screeners. They can't really do anything that you can't do in the computer age.
- They do not have your company's best interest at heart. Headhunters have a vested interest in throwing as many marginally qualified applicants at you as possible. They will not encourage you to a carefully review in search of excellence as much as they will create a sense of urgency to move on applicants because they want to get paid.

- They are very expensive and provide only one benefit: that you only have to deal with one individual in the early stages of the selection process instead of many job candidates. But this is temporary, and you have to interview the people anyway.

FREE RECRUITMENT SOURCES

Don't overlook the virtually cost-free options you have right under your nose for publicizing your position. Level 4 is about learning to work smarter. Maximizing these resources will not only save you money but will target your search and save you hours of wasted time reading résumés and talking to unqualified applicants.

- **Personal and professional referrals.** One thing hasn't changed since the writing of the first edition of this book: the best source of leads for recruiting great salespeople is still your network of contacts. If your personal network is deficient, then you need to go back to Level 1 and begin making the contacts necessary for you to succeed in your role as a sales recruiter. Ask your friends for the names of sharp up-and-coming people they know. It doesn't matter if the people they recommend are looking to make a job change or not. You can build an inventory of talented people to contact from colleagues and friends you know and respect. Warm leads are always better than cold ones.

  Friends aren't the only people in your sphere of influence. Our lives are populated with many outstanding people in their fields, all of whom could be a storehouse of potential leads. Talk to your banker, your insurance agent, your accountant, and any other professional you know and trust. Describe what you're looking for in a phone call, e-mail, or personal note to them. Attach a copy of your sizzling recruitment ad (more on how to write great recruitment ads in the next chapter). If these professionals give you a referral, ask permission to use their names. You intensify your recruiting appeal considerably if you can introduce yourself to a prospect by saying, "I was talking to

John Smith at the bank the other day, and he tells me how much you impress him. I'd like to talk to you about an opportunity."

There are many online networking sources available to you. The largest is LinkedIn.com, with two hundred million members.

Regardless of what kind of selling or recruiting you do, there's absolutely no substitute for personal and professional networking.

- **Local professional organizations.** Here's another frequently overlooked source of free contacts: professional and service organizations in your community. Civic clubs and social groups offer space on bulletin boards and in their newsletters. Don't overlook women's professional groups as well as the traditional service clubs. Offer to help a few people in these organizations find work. Religious groups (churches, synagogues, fraternal organizations, etc.) are another fertile field for leads. Larger congregations may sponsor programs in which members from the congregation with consulting and recruiting experience help people in the community find employment. Pastors, priests, and rabbis know good people in their congregations who may be looking for exactly the opportunity you are offering.

- **Local schools and institutions of higher learning.** One of our long-time clients is doing more than 50 percent of their recruiting at local colleges and universities. They have been recruiting on campus for eight years. Of the thirty-four graduates they hired, thirty-two are still with the firm. This compares to a 45 percent retention rate for the industry. They sell on average $480 per day more than other recruits. Of course, this option is going to work best for entry-level sales positions rather than positions that require a lot of sales experience. Even if the school doesn't offer a specific degree in selling, many schools offer career counseling and job-placement services to their graduates. Visit local campuses. Get to know the people in charge of job placement. Ask about job fairs and other appropriate ways you can work with these campuses to publicize your opportunity. At the very least, ask to post your recruitment ad on a bulletin board.

- **Public employment bureaus.** Visit the folks at your local or state employment service. Many of these offices are connected to the US Employment Service and provide hiring resources to businesses like yours. Your only outlay to tap into this vast network is a little time and effort.

- **Major employers in your community laying off workers.** Merger mania, downsizing, and reorganizations create corporate instability in the marketplace. Companies forced to retrench usually lay off based on issues of seniority; last hired, first fired. Many of these low-tenured reps could be quality employees. Frequently, these firms hire outplacement specialists who look for community partners to help employees find new work. Identify yourself to these professionals and be sure to include them in your recruitment network.

WHAT ABOUT RECRUITING YOUR COMPETITORS' REPS?

This question frequently comes up in our work and invariably prompts a great deal of discussion both pro and con. There is no simple answer. Our opinion is that your best strategy concerning recruiting competitors' reps will depend on your industry and your management style. Highly specialized positions requiring experienced candidates virtually guarantee some employee raiding.

One manager in the credit card services industry tells about an interesting tactic. He shall remain anonymous for obvious reasons. He answers the ads of his competitors, pretending to be looking for a job. He says it gets him in front of experienced people (yes, the people interviewing him for the job) who are often surprisingly eager to learn of a better opportunity when they discover the true purpose for his appointment. Not everyone could carry off this bit of chutzpah, but it works for him. You probably won't be surprised to know that his management style is that of a controller-performer. Recruiters with high control needs find guerilla techniques like this immensely satisfying.

Going behind enemy lines has pluses and minuses. On the plus side, you not only find experienced salespeople with contacts, but you temporarily deal your rival a severe setback by stealing a productive player off the opposing team. On the negative side, you may create legal tangles for yourself if the salesperson is encumbered by a noncompete clause in the previous employment contract. There's no guarantee that a top salesperson in one organization will automatically repeat his or her success in your company. Successful selling involves more than just the selling style of the rep. The previous environment may have supplied a more compatible management style, corporate culture, business climate, etc. The practice will drive up your costs. Going after someone who already has a good job means that you will only be able to woo them away with a much larger investment than it might take to hire someone who has come looking for you. Finally, another negative is the ill will created within your industry or specialization that might backfire on you one day if you found yourself working with or for the person you upset. Raiding the competition's talent is done every day. But remember—what goes around comes around.

CONCLUSION

In a market where there are fewer jobs than people looking for work, we recommend staying away from paid sources of leads such as Internet job sites, newspapers, and headhunters. They may help you collect a lot of résumés, but the applicants they attract will seldom have the initiative of candidates uncovered through your own free sources of leads. These include:

1. Personal and professional referrals
2. Schools and universities that offer job fairs and placement services
3. Local civic and religious groups

4. Public employment bureaus
5. Outplacement specialists

We also discussed the pros and cons of recruiting people away from competitors. In general, we think the negatives outweigh the positives of such a practice, especially in a job market that favors the recruiter.

14

HOW TO WRITE A SIZZLING RECRUITMENT AD

The best way to learn about writing a good recruitment ad is to spend time reading and analyzing recruitment ads. Go to the Internet job sites and find sales jobs. As you browse, pay special attention to the ads that immediately catch your eye. Why are these notices more attention grabbing than other ads? Why do you read some and skip over others? Do some ads seem to have more credibility than others? Learning to create a sizzling recruitment ad is a Level 4 skill that few recruiters can overlook.

ELEMENTS OF SIZZLING ADS

Sales ads have many components, and each component works to attract the right candidate. Never forget that the purpose of your ad is to find qualified candidates who match your needs, not to generate résumés. Consider the following aspects of size, design, message, and call to action when designing your ad.

SIZE MATTERS

Before candidates read one word of your ad, they've already formed an opinion of your company from the appearance and size of your notice. In recruitment ads, the media is the message.

Ancient artists were required to paint kings larger than life. To modern eyes, the perspective of this art seems all wrong. But those primitive monarchs knew bigger was better, or at least more important. People instinctively look first at what is largest on the page. It's the way our brains work. It's also the way classified ads work. In most newspapers, larger job notices get placed first. So, when both size and position work for you, your ad screams, "This is important! I'm willing to pay for the best! Pay attention to me!"

LEVERAGE THE BRAIN'S INTUITIVE RESPONSES

The first step is getting your ad noticed by leveraging the brain's intuitive responses. Along with size, the appearance of your ad either invites or repels readers. Our brains intuitively dislike complexity and confusion. Most people will be more attracted to your ad if you don't cram too much information into it. Empty space is more attractive to the brain than clutter. Notice the use of white space in the employment ads that caught your eye. If you must include a lot of fine print in your ad, be sure your headline and your main recruiting points stand out by surrounding them with white space.

Another way to get your ad noticed is to include artwork or photos. When scanning a page of information, the human eye is conditioned to look at faces first. Until you can afford a big-name celebrity endorsement, you may not have famous faces to draw attention to your ads. That's okay. Any photo of smiling, attractive people will be more likely to get noticed than ads without pictures of people. However, the kind of picture you include will target your appeal to the exact selling style you may be trying to reach (more about that in a moment).

One company tripled the response rate to its recruitment ad simply by adding its corporate logo. The logo wasn't particularly artistic or noteworthy. As with faces, in a page full of words the brain intuitively goes to symbols. Surrounding the logo with white space draws the eye to it. The brain is always looking for clues to simplify the chaos coming at it from the environment. The brain directs attention first of all to large symbols before trying to interpret small ones (such as words).

Another trick to grab attention is to reverse the background to black and use white text. This intuitively draws the brain more than the ordinary black text on white background.

MATCH VALUES TO NEEDS

So far we haven't said anything about the message of your recruitment ad. The omission is intentional. Usually it's the case that the words you use to get attention are secondary to the size, placement, and attractive design of the ad. If prospects don't notice the ad and gain a positive impression of what you have to offer, the chances of their actually reading the content is quite small. If the design doesn't match the copy, your credibility suffers and the response rate plummets. Once you've got the reader's attention, your ad needs to sizzle if you're going to sell the reader.

Let's revisit what we've learned about why people buy things. Sales happen when you fill a need with something the customer is convinced has value. That means that before any sale takes place, three things have to happen:

- *You have to be in front of a customer.*
- *You have to know what the customer needs.*
- *You have to persuade the customer of the value of your product or service to satisfy that need.*

Let's apply these same three principles to writing a great recruitment ad.

1. Decide who your audience is. This will to a large extent dictate where and how your ad will get in front of prospective salespeople. Once you know whom you're trying to reach, you'll have a much better idea about how you can reach them.

2.	Next, determine the medium you will use. Today more often than not this means choosing a website on which to publicize your ad. What sites do the people you are trying to reach regularly visit? If you are advertising for a position in one location, you will want to include local sites as well as national job boards.

3.	Your ad must create a need or bring a subconscious need above the threshold of awareness. This means using images and words designed to meet the emotional needs of the viewer/reader.

4.	Your ad must persuade readers that what you have to offer will satisfy those needs. The deeper and more personal the need you address and satisfy, the more likely you are to generate a considered response. Tell candidates one or two unique facts about you, your company or product, and the work environment. Relate what differentiates you from your competition. Hammer these distinctive factors home every chance you get. You're further ahead stating one unique benefit about your opportunity (flexible hours, casual dress code, location of your company) than you are publicizing a laundry list of trumped-up hyperbole ("unlimited income," "chance of a lifetime," "easiest job you'll ever have").

5.	Publish the income range of the position as well as the type of compensation package (commission, salary plus bonus, etc.).

	•	"Commission only; average first-year income $38–42K."
	•	"Starting monthly draw during three months of training $3K; full commission thereafter."

Realistic income estimates will attract more genuinely qualified candidates. Overstated claims may entice some gullible folks to contact you, and you may even get some of them to sign up. But you come out ahead financially by telling the truth up front rather than incurring the high costs of job turnover from the disillusioned and disaffected. Remember—the purpose of the ad is to find candidates who match your needs, not generate a pile of résumés.

HOW RECRUITMENT ADS APPEAL TO THE FOUR STYLES

By now, you should be getting the idea that emotional needs are critical to trying to influence people. Hire Performance is the process of using emotional needs to demystify the process of influence. If your ad can subliminally addresses emotional needs, candidates will find your ad more enticing and will be more motivated to talk with you about your opportunity. Additionally, you may dissuade some types of people from wasting your time by sending you résumés.

We know that emotional needs generate a person's selling style. Do you know what kinds of salespeople perform best within your selling environment? What selling styles do you most want to attract? If you can appeal directly or even indirectly to those emotional needs, your ad begins to sizzle.

If you are going to be the manager of the person you are attempting to reach, you must be certain that your ad doesn't merely reflect the preferences of your style and that it doesn't attract a style that is contradictory to your own. This mistake is often seen in companies that train their new hires in empathetic consultative sales but put out ads that appeal to self-starting, money-motivated, driven controllers. Those two needs don't coexist well. Something's got to give. More on that in the next section.

Professional recruiters must pay attention to how their emotional needs can skew their perception and negatively influence the objectivity of the interview process. Your selling style will help you attract some types of candidates to your job while putting off other types. If you're trying to build a winning team, you don't want everyone responding to your ad. If a baseball team desperately needs pitchers, scouts shouldn't be wasting time interviewing shortstops or outfielders. In the same way, you want the right people responding to your recruitment invitation. By specifically targeting emotional needs in your ad copy, you influence the kind of people who will respond. The small print can address the business need, but the subliminal message targets the values and social style of candidates. If the manager of the team you're recruiting for is a big-time control freak, you know you don't want to attract empathizers. Since some styles work well together and others can make sparks fly, writing a sizzling recruitment ad requires paying careful attention to the style cues you communicate. You want to attract people with styles and values that are compatible to manager's values and to the selling philosophy of the company.

If you're aware of your style, you know the kind of people with whom you are likely to work best and those who will frustrate you. Design words and pictures that appeal to the deep preconscious needs of those you want and need to attract.

CONTROLLERS

If you're looking for a strong closer, someone who can work without a lot of supervision, your recruitment ad should obviously *not* emphasize concepts like teamwork and cooperation. You're looking for someone with strong controller behavior, and these soft and fuzzy people attributes will mostly attract empathizers. Controllers respond best to ads that show pictures of tough people rather than smiling people. Use short sentences with punchy words. Shock value grabs the controller.

Here's an interesting discovery we've made about controllers and the ads they respond to: people with strong control needs seem to be intuitively attracted to a kind of negative advertising that actually dares them *not* to do something. Because they don't like to be told what to do, they actually are attracted to such bold phrases as "Don't read this ad unless you're one tough-minded closer who can handle responsibility that would destroy most salespeople." It's the challenge that excites the controller. Don't hesitate to appeal to their sense of duty and suspiciousness. Position your opportunity as demanding and difficult and be prepared for strong-willed people to show up on your doorstep.

Remember—you don't want to hire everyone who responds to a controller-friendly ad, but you are more likely to find a self-starting closer in that pool of candidates than in the general population who might respond to a plain vanilla ad.

PERFORMERS

If you need a salesperson to make a powerful first impression and tell your story, you want an ad that will attract performers with appeals to recognition, prestige, and glamour. Include pictures of young, energetic, well-dressed, laughing people in your ad. Always start the ad with the word "YOU" in large, bold letters. There's nothing more important to the performer. Appeal to their sense of fun. Position your opportunity as prestigious, with lots of opportunity for recognition. Performers are drawn to money because to them it represents the enjoyment of life. Here is an example of an ad that should attract performers: "You can have a blast marketing our world-renowned product to high-end homeowners. If you're an energetic, dynamic free thinker, we want to see you." Notice the emphasis on status and visual language. Performers want to be seen.

ANALYZERS

If you are looking for salespeople who are careful and conscientious, or if you work within a highly regulated industry, your ad will likely need to target people with analyzer tendencies. Analyzers are attracted to ads that ask questions rather than make statements—ads that include lots of facts and figures, graphs and charts, maps and details. These satisfy their emotional need for information. Small print acts like an aphrodisiac for analyzers. Consider positioning your opportunity as a problem to be solved. Be sure to mention benefits and company stability, as many analyzers also have a strong need for stability. Here's an example of what we mean. "Are you looking for salary plus bonus plus benefits? We're a solid, stable company looking for an expert to solve our customer's problems."

EMPATHIZERS

If you need a salesperson to build relationships and service existing accounts, appeal to empathizers by emphasizing things like teamwork and personal caring in your ads. Use inclusive words like "us" and "our." Soften the hard edges. Use pictures of people working together and smiling. Example: "Our close-knit team needs a people person to provide customer care and invite new clients to partner with our company."

The more you know about your selling style and the kind of relational skills necessary to sell your product or service, the better, more effective ad you'll write. By targeting emotional needs, your ad can communicate at a subliminal level that will target and strengthen the appeal to your ideal candidate.

EEOC GUIDELINES

Be careful to avoid mentioning anything in your ad about race, religion, color, gender, age, physical abilities, or other factors that may be considered discriminatory. Not only are such biases illegal in today's workplace, but they are also bad for business. Be sure any and all requirements outlined in your recruitment ad are clearly job related. Keep the focus on what people *do,* not what they *are.* If you satisfy these requirements you likely qualify to end your ad with the phrase "Equal Opportunity Employer."

ACTION LINE

Perhaps the most important part of any recruitment ad is the call to action. What is it you want prospective candidates to do? The action line needs to be spelled out clearly and precisely.

You have five basic action choices:

    come
    call
    fax
    e-mail
    mail

What your ad asks candidates to do predicts the kind and quality of response you get. Your action line can work for you or against you. If you want to get a lot of responses, publish a fax number or an e-mail address and ask for résumés. These action lines require the least initiative or commitment from job seekers. Asking candidates to mail résumés ups the ante a little, as the job seeker must invest the price of a postage stamp and a trip to the mailbox. But give the rainforests a break and cut down on the paper. Don't ask candidates to call unless you are using voice mail to screen applicants for a job involving a lot of telephone work. Answering calls from an ad is a huge time and energy trap, especially if you're a small firm. You can't interview and take calls at the same time. There are other, less-obvious problems with this method as well. What if a good candidate gets sent to voice mail or gets lost in "phone hell" (press 1 for this, 2 for that). Again, a knowledge of the styles helps predict responses. Controllers hate automated phone systems. Performers give up if it's too complicated. A lot of good salespeople could fall through the cracks. We made this point previously but it bears repeating: try to always relate your ad's call to action to the skills and initiative required by the job. The more commitment your action line requires, the fewer responses you get. But the candidates who do respond will usually be of much better quality. Asking a candidate to show up in person not only weeds out those with little initiative, it also says right up front that initiating contact is the most important skill required for success in this position.

In general, your action line should avoid asking for résumés. Sure, everybody wants to see a good response from an advertising investment, but a blizzard of creative writing is hardly the best measure of an ad's success. In fact, the less your job requires writing and organizational skills, the less you should rely on written résumés. Asking sales candidates to send résumés elicits a lot of low-energy, low-commitment responses. It invites many of the merely curious to distract you from finding qualified candidates with more drive and initiative. You're hiring a salesperson, not a librarian. Use the hiring process to filter out the unmotivated and nonserious candidates.

CONCLUSION

Recruitment ads sizzle when they

- are specifically targeted to the right audience using the right media;
- use elements of design like white space effectively;
- bring emotional needs to the threshold of awareness and meet those needs by using key words and concepts targeted to the style of rep you want to attract; and
- employ an action line that utilizes skills essential for the job and also filters out the unmotivated.

15

HOW TO EVALUATE RÉSUMÉS

Reading and evaluating résumés is always part of recruiting a winning sales team, but we don't think you should rely too heavily on the résumé. Résumés are often constructed to conceal much more than they reveal. With a little help, though, you can dig out the critical information you need. This Level 4 recruiter skill is all about getting at the truth that all too often lies buried between the lines.

FIRST READ: THE SCAN SORT

Don't read all the résumés you receive. Your time is too valuable. Start by simply scanning résumés for one or two items that stand out. You can eliminate many candidates with a quick inspection of the résumé. You'll be able to discard many résumés with just a quick once-over. Some will be sloppy and unprofessional. Others will quickly reveal a person without enough experience or education. All the résumés that survive this initial scan sort can be prioritized later according to your hiring profile. Scan sorting is a skill you develop with practice.

Get three cardboard boxes. Label or color them green, yellow, and red. In the green box put all the résumés that pass your initial scan criteria. Toss your obvious rejects into the red box. The yellow box is for everyone else—"a definite maybe."

Don't bother printing e-mailed résumés. Scan sort them on your monitor. Don't waste time and resources when you don't have to. Instead of boxes, create folders on your computer into which you scan sort the résumés you receive. Scan the page quickly without getting bogged down in details.

Three rhyming words guide your initial résumé scan sort: neat, complete, and meet.

IS IT NEAT?

Neatness correlates highly with conscientiousness. Sloppy résumés point to someone who isn't careful or who didn't take the time to do something properly. If you sell a technically sophisticated product, a neat résumé can be a vital clue to spotting quality candidates. Since many online job services ask candidates to copy and paste résumés into their application, neatness must be defined a bit more broadly.

Neat also means correct. If your initial scan reveals obvious misspelled words and grammatical mistakes, you're looking at a candidate who is either in too big a hurry or who may require additional training.

IS IT CONCISE AND COMPLETE?

Long résumés usually mean one of three things.

1. The candidate is an exceptionally experienced individual responding to an ad that was overly general.
2. The candidate has a tough time focusing on priorities.
3. The candidate is likely an analyzer with out-of-balance information needs.

Unless you are trolling for skilled, experienced candidates, require résumés be concise, one-page summaries, if at all possible. However, be sure to tell candidates not to leave gaps in their employment history for the sake of brevity. Shorter résumés save you time and give you a clue about the candidate's ability to focus and set priorities.

Complete also means no gaps in employment history. Time gaps often mean something is being omitted or covered up. The candidate may not want you to know about what was happening during that time period. Spotting gaps does not require a lot of time spent reading details. If your quick scan reveals obvious missing information, don't put that résumé with your top candidates. If you are an analyzer, don't get bogged down in too many details, worrying that you'll miss something in a résumé. If it's worthwhile, you'll catch it later when you unpack the green and yellow boxes.

DO SKILLS AND BACKGROUND MEET YOUR CRITERIA?

Someone with experience in your industry might be a better candidate than a rookie with no background or training. However, don't assume that all experienced candidates automatically match your profile. You may need to explore the kind of training they received to determine if their selling skills are easily transferable. Similarly, you shouldn't be too quick to disqualify an applicant with a background that may not exactly fit the sketch of your ideal candidate. The yellow box is for those résumés that have caught your interest for some reason. It's not even important at the scan-sort stage for you to know why you put a résumé in the yellow box. Things can be interesting without necessarily being good or bad, right or wrong.

A quick way to determine if a résumé meets your scan-sort criteria is to look for the candidate's job objective. Not all résumés contain an objective, but those that do will usually put it right at the top of the page. Scan the career objective first. If it is obvious that the objective doesn't match the position you've got, dump it in the red box.

After completing your initial scan sort, save the résumés in the green and yellow boxes. Trash everything in the red box without a second thought (unless company protocols require differently).

SECOND READ: RÉSUMÉ MARKUP

The scan sort whittled down the task of résumé reading to a more manageable size. Now you're ready for a second read in what we call *the résumé markup.* Begin with résumés in the green box. If you are working with sorted e-mailed résumés, print the ones that belong in the green box. Put the yellow box aside for the time being. Your focus for the second read is only on those candidates who appear to be the closest match to your hiring objective.

Photocopy the résumés in your green box, because you're going to make comments and notations on the résumé. In other words, you're going to mark it up now to save you time later. Keep a clean original as backup. As you read the green-box résumés from candidates who made your initial cut, circle or highlight anything that leaps off the page at you. Positive or negative, it could be an important clue to the individual's values and selling style. Make notes of your concerns and questions in the margins of the résumé. You are not making any final decisions at this stage. You are just jotting down your impressions and questions. You're now ready to gather business intelligence on your candidates. Here are clues that emerge from typical sales résumés.

WORK AND EDUCATION HISTORY

Background and education can help you determine a couple of important facts about your candidate. Does the individual's background match the requirements you need? Does this person have experience with the kind of market your firm sells to? What does the candidate's education tell you about career aspirations? If your company sells insurance programs to high-value individuals such as doctors and lawyers, a candidate with only a year or two of college may not be the best fit. Work and education history can also provide a heads-up about the individual's stability. Did she finish school? How long did he stay at his previous jobs? Obviously, young people just beginning a career are going to show less workplace stability than sales veterans. If you spot a pattern of changing addresses or jobs every six to eight months with an experienced candidate, it's a pretty safe bet that this rep won't be around your company long either.

While we're on the subject, let's examine a question that many recruiters ask and upon which they disagree. How much mobility is too much? Some managers say a candidate who stays in any job for more than three or four years may not have enough initiative. We think this depends on the industry and the state of the economy. In the unprecedented growth market of the nineties, good candidates moved on every six months as opportunities exploded and businesses couldn't get enough workers. When jobs become scarce, prudent people are less likely to change jobs. As a rule, eighteen months to three years in a sales position is about average. If your candidate is changing jobs every six months to a year, you probably need to ask some questions about whether he or she gets bored quickly. Three years or more in an entry-level job or five years in the same managerial position may indicate complacency or risk avoidance. When you evaluate a candidate's experience, try to get a feel for the amount and types of training that may be required. The more you invest in training your sales team, the less you can afford to hire a job jumper.

HOBBIES

Hobbies listed on sales résumés generate a lot of disagreement among sales recruiters. Some see hobbies as a distraction from selling. Others believe that listing hobbies offers evidence of a well-rounded individual. We think both are probably right. If the candidate has included hobbies or outside interests in a résumé, there's a reason. For the inexperienced candidate, it may be to fill up space on the page. Or it could be a talking point your candidate wishes to raise in a potential interview. You gather two important pieces of intelligence from your candidate's list of hobbies: the degree of outside distractions to work and the energy level.

First, if your position requires long hours when starting up or demands working evening or weekend hours, shy away from candidates with hobbies involving ongoing commitments of time and energy. Coaching Little League, serving on the school board, or getting active in politics are wonderful avocations, but these hobbies play havoc when starting a new job or making a career change. They take huge blocks of time and often zap the energy and focus demanded by sales. Be sure candidate hobbies don't conflict with work. If job seekers are forced to choose between hobbies they've learned to enjoy and a new job, they may make some adjustments in the short run, but ultimately the hobbies win out.

Hobbies can also indicate a person's energy level. When it comes to top-producing salespeople, active hobbies like swimming, bike riding, or jogging help salespeople maintain higher energy levels. There's nothing wrong with someone who lists movies, computer games, reading, or other passive hobbies, but there's a strong correlation between active hobbies and career stamina. Circle the hobbies listed or make a note to ask about them in the interview.

TRACK RECORD

Be impressed with résumés that provide real sales numbers and not just titles and duties. Put these in the green box right away. Specificity is a strong sign that your candidate knows the importance of setting goals and being accountable for production. Even so, citing sales numbers is not necessarily proof that your applicant was directly responsible for such success. You will want to add a question for your interview: were these results an individual or a team effort? Still, a clearly spelled-out track record indicates that your candidate knows that sales is ultimately about the bottom line. Circle the sales numbers as a topic for follow-up.

VERBS

At the risk of sounding like an English teacher, you can learn a lot about a candidate by reviewing the verbs on the résumé. As you read the résumé, circle all the action words. Verbs express behavior. What do they communicate? Are the verbs active (sold, managed, led, built, etc.) or passive (assisted, learned, was exposed to, etc.)? Is the applicant action oriented or thinking oriented? Are the words you've circled the kinds of behaviors you need for a candidate to succeed?

TECHNICOLOR RÉSUMÉS

Okay, you're still rummaging through the green box. Read each résumé in that box several times. Use color markers to prep for the interview, circling or highlighting items that you want to talk about. Be careful to avoid using colors that could telegraph too much inside information to the candidate, like red for bad or green for good. Yellow works well for items that need clarification, such as gaps in the timeline, time-consuming hobbies, and questions about references. Yellow means "ask about this." Obvious pluses in the candidate's background and/or skills can be circled in light blue highlighter. He may live close by, so circle the address. If she worked in the industry for a number of years, circle it in blue. If the candidate shows good job stability, write "stability" in the margin and circle it with blue. Perhaps you'll spot obvious elements of a selling style. Make notes using A for analyzer, P for performer, C for controller, and E for empathizer. Scribbled in blue means that style could be a plus; written in yellow means it could be an area of concern that needs to be verified.

Don't forget about your own emotional needs and the biases they can create when reading and evaluating résumés. Controllers have a natural tendency to find lots of yellows and very few blues because they find it easier to criticize than to compliment. If you're a controller, discipline yourself to always make one blue mark for every yellow comment on your Technicolor résumés. Empathizer recruiters are just the opposite. They will use up four blue markers for every yellow one because they're more comfortable giving compliments than being critical. Their emotional need for approval generates a more accepting approach. Empathizers need the same discipline, one yellow for every blue highlighted remark. Analyzers are already getting into this, devising better colors, more colors, using different symbols. Be careful that you don't spend more time analyzing than interviewing. You don't get paid to R&D the perfect résumé coloring system. Your goal is Hire Performance. Performers are likely to find this all tedious and complicated. Attention-driven people are notorious for only hearing what they want to hear. They've relied on their intuitive social skills for so long that it's difficult for them to approach recruitment in any systematic way. If that's the case, this book might look good on the shelf next to all the rest of the unread bestsellers by celebrity gurus. Be alert to the implications of your style as you read résumés. Be honest with yourself. Honesty is your best bet for recruiting a winning sales team.

If you follow this system for reading, prioritizing, and color-coding résumés, it will be easy to know whom you should contact first. They are in the green box, and their résumés have more blue than yellow highlighting. Demote those with the fewest blue markings to the yellow box and forget about them for right now. Yellow stands for "backups." You are only interested in yellow-box résumés after you've exhausted all those in the green box. If you do need to dip into the yellow box in the future, start again with the Technicolor résumés. They stand out because you've already determined their value to your sales efforts. Unmarked résumés in the yellow box were your lower priorities from the initial scan sort. Don't forget that you may have more yellow-box résumés on your computer that you'll need to print.

The more résumés you receive, the more critical it will be to implement a systematic way of dealing with all that paper. Even if you're a small start-up operation and you receive only a few résumés, it's never too soon to start building the disciplines, habits, and skills that contribute to Hire Performance.

HOW TO CONTACT REFERENCES

Contacting previous employers has become increasingly problematic. Recent precedent-setting lawsuits leave employers legally vulnerable for unfavorable recommendations that may contribute to a candidate being passed over for a job. So the most you'll get from contacting previous employers is verification of the dates of employment and perhaps a job title. References supplied by most candidates are sanitized to include only people prepared to sing the candidate's praises. However, you can look at candidate references from a different angle to uncover some critical clues about potential performance. For example, is the candidate willing to provide references? If not, why? What kind of references are they? Are they personal or professional? Is there anyone from a previous place of employment on the list? If so, is it a supervisor or a friend? The absence of professional references could merely indicate a lack of experience, but it might also be a clue that the candidate did not leave a previous employer on the best of terms. We're not saying ignore the references. You need to check them out. Here are some tips that should help you avoid trouble and get the information you really need.

IDENTIFY YOURSELF AND THE PURPOSE OF YOUR CALL

"Hello, Mr. Jones, my name is ... I'm (your position) at (your company name). I'm calling because Joe Candidate listed you as a reference on his résumé." Then shut up and gauge the immediate reaction. Does the reference want to talk about the candidate? Is she open to your call? Does she sound excited and enthusiastic, or do you sense apathy, confusion, or restraint? Those first few seconds speak volumes about the quality of this reference.

Let's take Zachary's example. He called one of the references. "Sally SalesRep listed you as a reference and I'd like to talk with you. Is this a bad time?" Zachary asked.

"No," the voice on the other end of the phone said slowly.

Zachary confirmed that Sally had worked as a rep in the company for the past couple of years. Then the reference said, "Sally. Hmmm. Yea, I guess you could say she did pretty well. Good salesperson. Sure."

That slight hesitation, that little phrase "I guess," told Zachary more about the quality of the reference than anything he said. He was trying to talk himself into giving Sally a positive reference. The words were there, but not the enthusiasm.

Sometimes you have to listen to what's not being said.

BEGIN BY PUTTING THE REFERENCE AT EASE

You might say, "I'm merely following up on the references Joe provided, and I wonder if you would you feel comfortable telling me a little about how well you know Joe."

Include this step if you're calling on a small business owner, frontline manager, or any non-HR professional. These businesspeople must be a jack-of-all-trades. They have lots of good information, but they may have read an article about businesses getting in trouble for giving bad referrals. Sometimes they're just too busy to talk. In those cases, they'll usually ask you to call back. Be aware that many small businesses are wary about references because they fear getting themselves or the candidate in trouble. If you recognize any hesitation on the reference's part to speak openly or candidly, and the reference hasn't arranged a time to call back due to busyness, politely terminate the call. There's no way of knowing what that reluctance is really about. Don't let it color your opinion of the candidate. In general, references will only give you positive information. Don't embarrass them, or yourself, by putting them in situations where they are forced to speak negatively.

ASK OPEN-ENDED QUESTIONS

"I'm sure you know how important it is to follow up on references. Why do you think Joe included you on his list?"

Don't ask the reference directly for opinions about the candidate's personality, character, or personal preferences. Legally, you could be at risk if you use the reference's opinion to disqualify an individual from a job, so don't waste your time asking. You could expose the unwitting reference to similar legal issues if you were found to have induced them to give a negative reference for which they are held liable. If a former employer hesitates to speak openly or candidly, withdraw the questions about performance and simply confirm the dates of employment and inquire about the candidate's title when employed.

If a reference volunteers negative information about the candidate, affirm the absolute confidentiality of your conversation. Say something along these lines. "Thank you for volunteering that information. I want to reassure you that your opinions will be held in the strictest confidence and your recommendations are only one of several sources of information we're using to select a person for the position." Document your reply by keeping it on file with the résumé of the candidate for a year. You may wish to send it to your lawyer or legal department. Discuss the issue with competent legal counsel to be sure you handle all employment issues according to the laws of your state as well as federal regulations.

PREPARE FOR YOUR INITIAL INTERVIEW

The markup read of green-box résumés prepares you for the next step—your initial interview. You should be prepared for at least two interviews with every serious candidate. Three interviews is probably better. Study the résumés in your green box closely before your first interview (if possible). As you prepare for the in-depth interview, make notes. Write down questions you need to ask. Hopefully the insights gained from this book will make critical issues leap off the page at you. You've gone to a lot of effort to think through your needs, plan your strategy, and set standards. Don't throw it all away at this point in the hiring process by relying on intuition.

Sales managers agonize after investing time and money to train salespeople to master a skill that they immediately forget in the heat of a sales call. They train reps to follow a sales script to guide their presentation. They practice the script to perfection. But in the excitement of the actual sales call, they don't apply anything that they've learned. That's where you are right now in your quest for Hire Performance. It's time to transfer training into practice. You've worked out a plan in previous chapters, and now you've got to stick with it. You must be selective. Even if you receive a smaller response from your ad than you'd hoped, you can't rush into hiring just anybody. In fact, a minimal response means you have to be *more* selective, *more* careful about those who may at first appear to be your top candidates. Better to ask the tough questions now before you invite this person on your team and put him or her on the payroll. Remember, every salesperson you interview puts your reputation and the future of your enterprise on the line. Compromise now and risk delaying the chance to recruit a winning sales team.

CONCLUSION

Résumés can conceal as much they reveal. This chapter details a two-step process for getting at the information you need from candidate résumés.

1. Prioritize candidates by a brief scan-sort technique.
2. Markup top-priority résumés using a color marker system for identifying concerns and compliments you might use in an interview.

We also identified some techniques for getting what you really need from reference checks without putting you or the person you are talking to into a difficult and possibly litigious situation.

16

SOCIAL MEDIA AND OTHER SOURCES OF INFORMATION

Prior to the first face-to-face interview, most employers begin the process of trying to verify the information included on an applicant's résumé. People can say anything on a résumé, and a lot do. Due diligence requires that the employer investigate the truthfulness of a candidate's claims. There are more resources available than ever before for the recruiter to gather critical intelligence. Here are some of the more important sources of information to be sure your applicants are all they claim to be. *Note:* Be sure your employment application grants you permission to obtain this background information. Consult with an attorney on the legal language appropriate to your state.

BACKGROUND CHECKS

If you are a large enough employer, your company will specify the types of intelligence you can gather on any individual. If you are a small business or an entrepreneur on your own, you should consider using one of the many background-screening services available on the Internet. Not all of these providers are equally helpful. But you don't have time to scour the dozens of databases that these services scour to come up with their reports. Costs vary depending on which services you use and how much information you require. You'll want to choose one that is easy to use and provides the most accurate information. Google "best background searches" and you will find summaries and reviews of all the major providers. The typical background check should provide you with a person's name, current address, address history, criminal history, and financial history.

You'll want an FCRA-certified credit check. FCRA stands for Fair Credit Reporting Act (you can Google it for more information). A good credit report doesn't always indicate personal integrity, but it does at least point to someone who has enough of a work ethic to protect their credit rating. Bad credit, slow-pays, and judgments don't automatically mean that someone is a deadbeat. However, a poor credit rating can indicate someone who could be under financial pressure. Consider asking a question like "I notice that you've been under some financial pressure lately. Can you tell me more about that?" Listen for the degree to which the individual feels like they are in control or the degree to which they may feel desperate. Desperate people seldom turn out to be top producers.

Not all background-check services provide information on driving records. Even if it's an inside sales role, we think you should obtain a motor vehicle report. A good driving record usually indicates someone who is prudent and responsible. Numerous tickets and accidents should be a red flag that an individual may enjoy taking unnecessary risks or disrespects authority.

Another option not included in all background-check services is an employment history. We think that this is critically important. As discussed earlier, previous employers are not likely to share much meaningful information. Verifying employment dates can uncover gaps that may have gone unreported in the candidate's résumé or application. It's better to find out missing information before you hire the slick-talking candidate. Gaps in employment history are more critical in older applicants than candidates just out of school. If you notice a gap, ask the candidate about it. Many times applicants try to hide employers from which they were fired or with whom they did not get along. Try to reassure your candidate that you only need to verify dates of employment. Ask if there were any problems; then listen carefully. Does the explanation sound reasonable or fanciful? If you suspect that the candidate is still being less than honest about the disparity, you'll want to terminate the interview as soon as possible. Do not pressure candidates to reveal what they may be covering up. Make a yellow note on the résumé to ask the candidate to clarify the discrepancy with employment dates. There may be a simple explanation.

If educational degrees or certifications are necessary for the position, ask the applicant to furnish grade transcripts and certification documentation from the certifying company or agency. Photocopies of diplomas and certificates are no longer adequate, as these can be easily faked with sophisticated desktop-publishing software.

As of the date of this writing, only two major background search firms offer all these pieces of public record intelligence: FindOuttheTruth .com and BackgroundPi.com.

SOCIAL MEDIA

One of the greatest changes in the business of recruiting since the first edition of this book is the emergence of social media. Reppler is a company that monitors social media. In a recent study of three hundred recruiters, they found that 91 percent use social media as part of their background screening on applicants. The three largest social media sites used are Facebook (by 76 percent of the recruiters), Twitter (53 percent), and LinkedIn (48 percent). Almost half of recruiters do a social media search after receiving the résumé and before the first interview. Twenty seven percent wait until after the initial interview, while about 20 percent wait until after the second interview and before making an offer.

Seven out of ten recruiters have turned down applicants based on information found on their social media pages. Some people are notoriously lax about their online information sharing. According to Reppler, the top reasons for disqualifying a candidate based on social media research are:

1. Lied about qualifications (13 percent)
2. Posted inappropriate photos (11 percent)

3. Posted negative comments about a previous employer (11 percent)
4. Demonstrated poor communication skills (11 percent)
5. Posted comments about drug use (10 percent)

The news isn't all bad, however. The same number of recruiters said that a person's social media helped them reach a positive hiring decision. Here are the top ways that social media helped.

1. Gave a positive impression of their personality and fit within the organization (39 percent)
2. Profile supported their professional qualifications (36 percent)
3. Online profile showed the candidate was creative (36 percent)
4. Showed positive communication skills (33 percent)
5. Showed candidate was a well-rounded individual (33 percent)

You must be very careful about the kind of social media research you do. These sites carry both implicit and explicit information about a person's race, age, marital status, disabilities, and other illegal criteria for employment. Never request that an applicant give you his or her username and password to their social media sites. Several states have already introduced legislation making this a violation of privacy laws. Federal regulations are probably not far behind. We recommend that you avoid using personal sites like Facebook and Twitter and concentrate on some of the more business-oriented social media sites, such as LinkedIn .com, to gather information.

CONCLUSION

Online background-check services are the most cost-effective and accurate way to gather intelligence on your applicants. Use these to verify résumés and better manage the risk of hiring the wrong person. More and more companies are using social media as a source for gathering information. However, this requires special caution so as not to violate the applicant's privacy or to let discriminatory information color one's evaluation.

17

THE FIRST INTERVIEW

A recent survey of recruiters found that preparing for the first face-to-face meeting was the most anxiety-provoking part of their job. Analyzers and empathizers probably feel the most apprehension: analyzers because they never feel they have enough information to carry off a good interview and empathizers because they need to be liked so much they dread evaluating people and rejecting any candidate.

Does interviewing intimidate you? It shouldn't.

HOW EFFECTIVE ARE INTERVIEWS REALLY?

We think that many recruiters dread the interview stage because they convince themselves that the initial interview is the most important piece of the selection process. But first interviews can be confusing and their value easily overrated. Candidates who are well coached in interview skills erode the value of interviews. Job seekers may have more experience interviewing than the recruiter, especially if the manager is new at the job. Good candidates typically invest more time than managers preparing for the interview, reading books and getting inside information on the company. The Internet not only gives recruiters great tools for searching and screening but also gives candidates access to more information than ever before. The applicant sitting across from you may have studied body language, stress-management cues, how to effectively answer questions, how to dress, and many other tips in preparation for the first interview. Most recruiters probably aren't half as well prepared as the candidate is. If you are rushing into the interview without a coherent strategy or without having done your background checks, you probably should be nervous. Without proper preplanning, recruiters tend to overrely on the interview as the primary ingredient for their gut-feel approach to selection. Good planning minimizes the stress that accompanies the face-to-face meeting. If you know what to ask, how to ask it, and why you're asking, you should feel more in control as a professional recruiter.

Let's look at a couple of important factors as you plan the first interview:

1. Where to interview
2. How many interviews should I plan?

1. **Where to Interview**

The first issue to confront as you plan for the interview is *where* you should meet to interview applicants. This is probably a moot point if your company is large enough to have a dedicated HR department. But if you're a small business in which you are wearing several hats, you may need to think about where you conduct that initial conversation. If your office projects your values and image, meet on your turf. If you can't see your desktop for the clutter, or you operate out of an office in your home, it's best to choose a neutral site. Sometimes you may need to travel to another town or state to meet with prospective candidates. In these situations, turf issues become a bit more complicated.

Avoid restaurant meetings if you've never met the candidate before. It's not just the cost of drinks and a meal that could prove a liability. You may rule out an applicant within a couple of minutes, but now you're stuck until either the meal is over or you can make a graceful getaway. Hotel lobbies work well for initial interviews. Find a comfortable location away from the main flow of traffic to avoid distractions and interruptions. If you like the candidate, you can then suggest the interview continue over lunch.

As a general rule, recruiters should never meet a candidate for the first time at the applicant's home or office. The social dynamic is all wrong. The interviewer is put in the role of guest and the candidate as host. Professional interviewing requires that the interviewer be in the dominant social position. Otherwise the recruiter is less likely to be as assertive or inquisitive as the situation may demand. Similarly, the salesperson is put at a disadvantage because he or she is not able to demonstrate critical social skills required in the typical sales call where reps meets clients on their turf.

2. How Many Interviews

Here's a true story Dr. Barnett tells that illustrates two very important principles:

- The less turnover you can afford on your sales team, the more interviews with candidates you should plan.
- Never hire on the first interview regardless of how impressed you are or how pressured you feel to make a quick decision.

Barnett was recruiting salespeople in Houston. He ran a newspaper ad in the local paper promoting an informational meeting at a downtown hotel. He flew in the night before, got a good night's rest, and prepared his standard presentation. The next morning he found the assigned meeting room, set up the space, and with everything ready, sat down to wait for those who would heed the recruitment ad's call to action. No one showed. Barnett waited for an hour, then two. He was about to retrieve his displays and brochures when, at last, one well-dressed young man poked his nose inside the door.

"Am I late?" he said and laughed.

"Better late than never," Barnett said, trying to keep a positive demeanor. "Come on in and let me show you what you missed."

After having invested over $1,600 in plane tickets, hotel costs, and newspaper ads, not to mention his time, Barnett wasn't about to leave town with nothing to show for it. The prospect handed over his résumé and, nose lifted slightly in the air, introduced himself as D. Thomas Smith or some snobbish-sounding name. Based on the way he talked and arrived late, his flashy clothes, and the glamorous picture on the résumé, Barnett knew right away he was dealing with an out-of-balance performer whose style was probably not compatible with Barnett's own performer-controller tendencies.

D. Thomas talked nonstop about himself, his impressive contact list, his interests, and his legendary ability to sell. "He was a total jerk," Barnett says. "Everything I *didn't* want on my team, but I was desperate to show something for the investment of my trip. I kept thinking how my VP of sales would give me trouble if I came back with nothing to show for the trip but a stack of expense vouchers."

Getting a word in edgewise, Barnett started selling D. Thomas on the opportunity and explaining that he would need to complete a sales assessment.

"Oh," said the applicant with a dismissive wave of his hand, "I don't think that will be necessary. You see, the reason I was late getting here was that I had an interview with another company (a competitor of Barnett's), and they've already made me an offer. Now I think I'd rather work with your organization, but I don't have time to take your 'little test.' If you can't make up your mind today, then I'm really not interested."

The expert threw away his Hire Performance, allowing himself to be emotionally influenced away from the strategic plan. "His sales pitch wowed me," Barnett says. "I thought if D. Thomas can sell me in the interview, he could sell iceboxes to Eskimos. I hired him on the spot."

Six weeks later D. Thomas disappeared with a company-owned laptop, the price of which came out of Barnett's pocket. D. Thomas alienated one of the firm's biggest clients and was recruiting other reps in the sales organization to his next selling scheme. D. Thomas cost the company tens of thousands of dollars in wasted time, effort, and lost opportunity. It would have been far less expensive to rerun the ads and spend three or four more nights in the hotel. In fact, this author could have lived like a king for several months on the road for what it cost to hire the wrong person.

Make it an inviolable rule: never hire anyone on the first interview. The hiring interview is a lot like dating. When you meet someone for the first time, you're on your best behavior trying to impress the candidate, and the candidate is putting his or her best foot forward to win your approval. Now, this is hardly the kind of environment in which to make an objective decision worth tens of thousands of dollars, not to mention reputations and careers. Have the discipline to step back from any candidate who gives a great interview. Get your objectivity back. Review what you learned in the interview and how it squares with your Hire Performance strategy.

HOW TO HAVE A GREAT FIRST INTERVIEW

The first interview should be the shortest, taking between twenty and thirty minutes. The purpose of the first interview is to get a general overview of the individual's social skills and emotional needs that govern the kind of first impression he or she is likely to make on your customers. You should not be getting into a lot of details on your first interview. Here are eight things to do to make that first interview a positive, productive experience.

1. **Greet the candidate.**
Introduce yourself and put the candidate at ease with social chatter. Smile as you chitchat to build rapport. Make lots of eye contact. Thank the individual for coming. Ask if he or she had any trouble finding you. Gauge the amount of preliminaries to the social skills and needs of the candidate. Is he comfortable and relaxed meeting you? Is she friendly or formal? What selling-style behaviors immediately emerge? Performers shake hands robustly, speak forcefully, and are excessively good-natured and highly expressive. Controllers will come across more self-controlled and matter-of-fact. Analyzers may smile (they usually do not laugh or show their teeth when they smile), are less expressive, and may appear to be slightly anxious and more formal than other types. Empathizers speak somewhat softly, smile genuinely, shake hands with less firmness, and nod their heads yes as you talk to them. If you suspect controller or analyzer tendencies, minimize the small talk and get on with the meeting. Performers and empathizers are likely to go on chatting for as long as you let them.

2. **Provide a brief overview.**
Transition to the business at hand by briefly proposing an agenda.

Summarize the process: that today's conversation will be somewhat brief, that the purpose is to begin to talk about the opportunity, and that a second, more comprehensive interview will follow if there's interest in doing so. Analyzers need the structure, so give them details about how much time you expect to take. Controllers and performers will have already started to hijack the control of the meeting away from you by both conscious and subconscious strategies, so it's important that you regain the initiative and maintain control of the interview. The simplest way to do this is to provide a simple verbal checklist of what's going to happen in the first interview and how long it should take. Do not give the impression that everyone gets a second interview, and don't mention anything about assessments at this stage.

3.   **Ask the candidate to complete a job application.**
If you haven't already completed this step, get the application done right away. Do not delay or allow the candidate to distract you from completing this step. Not only can you clarify information that may have been omitted from the candidate's résumé, but you also protect yourself legally. A résumé is not a legal document. The properly prepared job application is legally binding. Misleading statements on a job application give you a legal footing if you have to dismiss the employee later. The employment application should ask not only for basic biographical information (name, address, and phone number) and work history but should include statements granting permission for you to contact references, conduct credit checks or drug screens, and proceed with any other necessary investigative activity. Sample applications can be obtained from your state employment office. Your attorney can advise you on the specific appropriate language to satisfy state law and meet appropriate EEOC guidelines. When the candidate signs and dates the application, you have a legal document.

The candidate should complete the employment application in private. You should leave the room or interviewing area as the candidate completes the application, or you may prefer to usher the job seeker to another location with instructions to bring the application to you when finished. Work out in advance how you will handle the privacy issue, particularly if you are meeting the candidate at a neutral site.

Quickly scan the application in the same way you learned to scan résumés. Look for the obvious things first: neatness, completeness, gaps, and most important—*is it signed and dated?* If you received a résumé prior to the first interview and you prepared for this applicant, you should be able to quickly verify any items you highlighted in yellow on the résumé.

4. **Ask a general question about the candidate.**

Most job interviews we've endured start with one of two questions (sometimes both): "Tell me a little about yourself" and "Where do you see yourself in five years?" The well-prepared applicant expects these questions and is probably prepared with an answer. Starting the interview with a broad question like this gives the candidate a chance to get over any nervousness and adjust to the interview situation. These are not throwaway questions. Be sure you listen, as you can pick up valuable clues about the person's communication skills and selling style in these first few moments of social interaction. Although it takes some practice, professional interviewers learn to listen at two levels simultaneously. Not only do they need to evaluate *what* the candidate is saying but also *how* she is saying it. So listen to the content of the response. Where does she start describing herself? Does he talk about self more than relationships, education more than experience? What a person says first is a strong indication of personal priorities and values.

But don't get so focused on content that you miss the meta-communication; that is, how the candidate is saying it. Does the response seem canned or rambling? Are answers coherent or not clearly thought out? Does the candidate talk too much or not enough? Can you understand him? Is her self-presentation appropriate to the product or service you sell? At this early stage, discipline yourself to not criticize either what is said or how. Give only positive feedback to the candidate's self-presentation.

5. **Describe the position briefly, and tell the candidate something about the company.**

Talk about the main duties of the job. Describe the title of the person to whom the position is accountable, along with a general picture of the qualifications required for the job. Here's an example: "Lee, XYZ Widgets needs a direct sales rep in our North Carolina region to service our current customers and at the same time develop new accounts to build our market share. The North Carolina rep position reports to our eastern regional sales manager who is based in Richmond, Virginia. The skills that we've determined are critical to succeed in this position are strong communication skills, prospecting, problem solving, and at least two years of experience in direct sales." As you speak, pay attention to how well the candidate listens. At least half of selling is listening. Does the candidate interrupt? Ask questions? Clarify? Probe? Quickly lose interest?

If, on the basis of a negative first impression, you have already made the decision not to hire the individual, use the interview as an opportunity to create positive PR for your firm and to sharpen your skills. Instead of talking about the position, you might describe the company's growth and position in the marketplace. Don't immediately terminate an interview the moment you decide the job seeker is unqualified. Treat everyone with patience and respect. Develop habits that keep doors open. After all, you never know where you might meet again or whom the applicant knows.

6. Ask the candidate broad open-ended questions.

After clarifying that the applicant understands the position and the skills you are looking for, begin asking your preplanned questions. These are probes identified by your blue and yellow highlighting of the résumé. Ask general behavior-based questions about experience in the skills you identified as important to the job (more on that in chapter 19). Ask about strengths as well as concerns you have. Have the applicant talk about successes as well as challenges. Remember: your goal for the first interview is to assess the general skills required and the initial impression the applicant makes.

7. Answer the applicant's questions.

Ask if your interviewee has any questions. Aggressive candidates may want immediate feedback about their performance or where they stand in relation to others you have interviewed. Be honest about strengths but somewhat guarded about sharing your impressions of weaknesses. Don't give away too much information about whether or not there are other candidates, the salary or commission structure, or your hiring deadlines. If pressured for an answer, you can say you have other interviews scheduled and provide a general time frame for reaching a decision. Depending on your behavioral style, you may initially react negatively to candidates who pressure you, but what does this assertiveness say about the benchmarks of contactability?

Be wary of any candidate whose primary interest in the first interview is money. There's nothing wrong with applicants wanting to know about the general pay range or inquiring about benefits, especially if you don't publish the pay structure in your recruitment ad. However, the candidate whose interest in the job is pegged only to compensation is a red flag for us. Reps who are primarily money motivated will be the first to leave your company for a better offer.

8. Decide on next steps.

If the interview has not gone well, you will want to conclude it at an appropriate point. Give your well-rehearsed "Don't-call-us-we'll-call-you" speech. You might explain that you have several more candidates to interview and provide the general time frame in which the hiring decision will be made. Thank the candidate for coming and promise that you'll be in touch about any next steps, should they be necessary. We suggest that you always write a thank-you note or send an e-mail to candidates you have interviewed and turned down. That communication should affirm their skills and aptitude (after all, they did convince you to interview them) and inform them that the position for which they were applying has been filled. You may want to keep their résumé on file and tell them so. Wish them well and thank them for their courtesy and professionalism.

If the first interview has gone well and the candidate matches your Hire Performance criteria, review with your prospect the next steps in your recruitment process in more detail. Explain the multiple-interview process. Never mention a second interview until you know you're interested in pursuing the candidate further.

If you use a hiring assessment tool (like SalesKey), explain that you'll be administering a questionnaire as one of several tools (along with checking references and a second interview) to help you evaluate whether the job is the right fit for the individual. Make the context the fit of the job to the person, not the fit of the person to the job. This not only affirms the candidate but also builds positive professional regard in both interviewee and interviewer. If you want your candidate to complete the selection test at home, give the prospect a test booklet and answer sheet to take with him. Review the instructions briefly and tell your candidate how and when to get the results to you for scoring. If the assessment is not to be taken home, arrange, if at all possible, for the candidate to complete the questionnaire at the end of your first interview. Should this be inconvenient for your candidate, arrange a time when the assessment can be completed. The candidate should complete any profile in private.

You'll need a ready-made answer if the candidate asks about receiving a copy of the test results. Your policy about giving out assessment results will depend a lot upon the assessment you use. General assessments (such as personality or temperament profiles) have more potential for misunderstanding and mischief than highly targeted ones (core competency tests). This is because general tests are more subjective and can be discriminatory if they present a picture of the way somebody "is." Skill assessments tend to be more objective and less threatening to the candidate. Our general rule of thumb is that we do *not* share test results but rather will interpret results in general terms. We'll explain much more on assessments in the next chapter.

Schedule your next interview after you have received the results of the assessment and have had ample time to review references and other information sources. Schedule sixty to ninety minutes for the second interview.

CONCLUSION

First interviews should be brief, general, information-gathering events conducted on your turf. You're trying to determine the kind of first impression this candidate is likely to make with your customers. You also need to generate a legal employment application and, if you use an assessment, make arrangements for the applicant to complete the questionnaire before the second interview. Although interviews are not always effective in uncovering sales talent, a well-planned, professional first interview can be a positive first step toward building a winning sales team.

18

USING SALES-HIRING TESTS

Do a Google search on "sales-hiring tests" and you'll discover 143,000,000 results in less than half a second. There are so many brands, types, and styles of assessments that this chapter can only scratch the surface of the subject.

In our experience most recruiters plug sales assessments into the hiring process after a successful first interview. By this time the interviewer has formed a positive opinion about the job seeker and wants to validate that perspective with some objective information. Hiring tests given after an initial interview are called "postscreens." Questionnaires administered before the interview are referred to as "prescreens." Today's technology is drastically changing not only how hiring tests are given but when and why as well. In the days of paper-pencil hand-scored tests, recruiters had to meet with candidates face-to-face first before giving them the questionnaire. Then they might have to wait a week or more before they received results. Today, hiring tools are available 24/7 anywhere in the world via the Internet. Web-based, paperless selection assessments allow recruiters to prescreen candidates by sending them to an Internet site to complete a hiring profile and receive results before the first interview.

We developed SalesKey Pre-Screen to be much more cost efficient for recruiters than old-fashioned postscreening. By providing a link in the ad to collect the candidate's résumé and seamlessly administering the SalesKey questionnaire, sales managers don't lose time dealing with people who don't meet their basic profile. Recruiters gain a huge advantage by having objective information before the first meeting; that way they can use the first interview to zero-in on specific productivity issues. Prescreening can easily reduce by half the amount of time needed for interviewing. Postscreens may save some money on the cost of assessments if they are given only to individuals prequalified by an interview.

FIVE OBJECTIONS TO USING HIRING TESTS

In this chapter, you'll learn about two basic kinds of sales-hiring tests and why either one could undermine your Hire Performance. But first, we need to address the basic question of why you might want to use any sales-selection assessment. Since the first edition of this book, there appears to be much less hesitation among recruiters to utilize assessments. Despite their popularity, some recruiters refuse or hesitate to use sales-hiring tests. Here are the objections we hear most and our best attempt to answer them.

Objection #5—"I don't need it."
The truth is that every recruiter uses some type of selection test. Selection tests aren't necessarily limited to a page of multiple-choice questions. Take, for example, the selection test used by retail giant John Cash Penney. His recruitment strategy included taking potential managers to lunch or dinner. Not only would he learn a great deal about their social poise, but J. C. Penney was also convinced that he could discern important qualities of their potential management style. During the meal, Penney watched to see if the candidate seasoned food before tasting it. He thought anyone too quick with salt and pepper might also be too impetuous for Penney's more cautious style. J. C. Penney's hiring test might not satisfy EEOC standards today, but his methodology illustrates how veteran recruiters and managers, over a career of hiring decisions, develop informal indicators of talent. Experience leads them to trust certain marker behaviors. How a candidate dresses, the

accent of an applicant, the job seeker's hairstyle; these and many more individual preferences become a kind of selection criteria. The real issue is whether the selection test used by the recruiter is subjective or objective, validated or purely fanciful. One recruiter told Robinson that he never hires anyone with a beard or mustache. "Never had one that worked out," he said. That's his selection test! He is convinced that facial hair in some way predicts productivity!

What about you? Do you have informal selection criteria? Your personal style will predispose you to specific informal measurements used to evaluate applicants. Performers size up candidates on the basis of personal appearance or the kind of car the applicant drives. Empathizers judge on the basis of eye contact or quickness at building rapport. Controllers sometimes assess candidates on the basis of the person's decisiveness and self-confidence. Candidates with a good vocabulary impress analyzers. We know that good producers are a balance of all these attributes. Consequently, recruiters with balanced emotional needs are most likely to use informal assessments to best advantage.

Formal sales-selection tests are designed to deliver validated factual information. You can't always rely on your gut feel about an applicant. While every recruiter develops professional sensitivities, it is important to be clear about the criteria used to evaluate sales candidates. Recruiters who say they don't need selection tests are often intuitive, information-avoidant amateurs who are either too impatient to learn how to use a selection tool or vain enough to believe they are God's gift to staffing.

Objection #4—"I don't believe that sales tests can predict success."
To be honest, this objection seldom gets expressed exactly this way. More often it surfaces as, "I used such-and-so sales test and it didn't really help." As you can imagine, not all of those 143,000,000 "sales-hiring tests" are going to be equally helpful. In fact, most are a complete waste of time and resources. Sometimes an assessment doesn't work because it's built on faulty theory. In the early 1900s you might have invested in a phrenometer to help you recruit salespeople. Dubbing the product as "the latest in scientific research," this device measured the contours of a person's head. The size and placement of cranial contusions, it was thought, held the secret to predicting success.

Many assessments are still trading on studies carried out in the 1920s that described salespeople as outgoing, talkative, money motivated, and driven. Arthur Miller's Willie Loman in *Death of a Salesman* became the stereotype of the salesman. Beginning in the 1950s, personality assessments became the accepted standard for assessing career productivity. Today the most popular type of sales assessment is the sales-personality test. Unfortunately, there is little to no scientific evidence that personality predicts success. Sales careers have always tended to attract extroverts primarily, and by sheer force of numbers, success in sales became identified with outgoing, sociable personalities. Many so-called sales tests are really old-fashioned temperament assessments, based not on scientific discovery but on the ancient Greek theory of body fluids (sanguine for a person with too much blood, melancholy for a person with too much bile, etc.). These typologies are fun as parlor games but are little better than a coin toss at predicting successful salespeople. Don't get us wrong. These personality and temperament tests can and do measure all kinds of interesting things. But if there's no proven correlation between what a test measures and one's ability to sell, it's as useless as a swizzle stick to a teetotaler.

SalesKey is not a personality test. It measures behaviors; specifically, behaviors that help or hinder contact initiation. SalesKey does a lousy job of predicting success in sales organizations where salespeople do not initiate contact with prospective buyers or current clients. But in organizations where prospecting and client contact are important aspects of sales success (which our research indicates is the most critical behavior to sales success in direct sales), SalesKey is a highly accurate tool to help forecast productivity.

The lesson here is this: before you use any sales-hiring test, you must have objective evidence that what a test measures is directly linked with sales productivity. This information should be included in the technical manual of any reputable assessment.

Objection #3—"Tests are hard to understand. I don't want to become an amateur psychologist."
Every manager is, or quickly becomes, an amateur psychologist, whether he or she wants to be or not. Ultimately, managing is a people business,

and psychology is the study of why people behave the way they do. If you're good with people, you stand a better chance of being a good manager and recruiter. We don't disagree—some tests can be hard to understand. In fact, some assessments are intentionally complicated to obfuscate their lack of scientific pedigree. But as with any tool, most reputable assessments will train users in the proper use of their tools. Some tests are hard to understand because human behavior itself is so fickle and full of vagaries. Any test designer will tell you that it's a challenge to have a test that is both scientifically precise and user friendly. The first version of SalesKey was huge and complicated. Preliminary statistical analysis proved very promising. The scientists and statisticians loved it. Unfortunately, sales managers couldn't understand it. So, it was back to the drawing board again and again to synthesize scientific reliability with real-world practicality.

Objection #2—"Tests are too expensive and just add to the cost of hiring."
This objection is being heard less and less from sales organizations as the cost of hiring the wrong person can easily escalate well into six figures. Testing candidates for a sales position can save you money in three significant ways.

1. *Sales tests can save you the cost of a bad hire.*
   In the first edition of our book, we cited a research study of more than twenty companies. The average cost of a bad hire was about $25,000. Today that cost approaches twice that much. Based on that study, using SalesKey as a hiring tool would have improved sales productivity in the sample by 45 percent overall and saved $273,450.00 in bad hiring costs, making the average SalesKey assessment worth $5,411.76. That represents an average return on investment (ROI) of 4,832 percent. A validated sales selection test like SalesKey is worth literally its weight in gold for the typical direct-sales organization. Here's a simple rule for weighing the value of a sales-hiring assessment. Figure the cost of a sales-hiring mistake, including lost opportunity (the money you would have made if you had hired a good salesperson). If

you can pay less than .01 percent of your bad hire cost for a selection test, it's a bargain. Consider it an insurance premium to help indemnify you against the loss of bringing a sales dud on board.

2. *Sales tests can drive down the cost of training.*
   Hiring right in the first place means that your training programs can be informational rather than transformational. Transformational training is the most expensive kind. Transformational training requires that you gauge your curriculum to the lowest common denominator of sales inexperience and run everybody through the same cookie-cutter program. In most cases, you end up wasting valuable time and resources trying to transform civilians into a sales force. Informational training, on the other hand, is targeted to the specific needs of each recruit. This individual approach is not only faster and more cost efficient but promotes morale because informational training is less likely to alienate or frustrate sales veterans. Experienced reps new to a company may only need product knowledge, information about administrative details, and perhaps a little remedial training in the unique skills necessary to your marketing approach.

   Speaking of veterans, testing can lower training costs by giving you a clearer picture of the veteran salesperson's skill level and personal issues. Just because someone has experience in your industry doesn't mean it was good experience. She may have learned bad habits that will impair her ability to be productive in your organization. She may have developed a blind spot to issues critical to success with your clients. Assessments can provide extremely helpful information for developing the talent of your people.

3. *Sales tests can help reduce turnover.*
   Hiring the right people not only impacts the bottom line by hiring better salespeople and lowering training costs but also contributes to lower turnover rates. People who fit well with

the organization and sell a lot are happier and tend to hang around longer than employees whose style doesn't match the team or selling environment. Good salespeople want to sell, not sit through hours of indoctrination or remedial training. The right kind of testing allows you to identify people with selling skill sets already in place. The reps who can get up and running rapidly not only help you recover your recruitment costs more quickly but improve profitability by taking less time and energy managing emotional and productivity issues.

Another way sales assessments reduce turnover and save money involves team dynamics and selling style. Some sales assessments identify the kind of manager who will most likely work best with the candidate. For example, let's say your assessment diagnoses that your new salesperson is somebody who needs to be in control of his own time and doesn't work as well on a team as on his own. Assigning such an individual to a touchy-feely manager is a prescription for disaster. Some reps will develop beautifully in a customer-oriented consultative-sales approach. They will begin to progress almost instantaneously, while others will want to close sales quickly. Geeks need to sell technical stuff and can become unglued when they don't get facts and figures. Conversely, put a prima donna performer under the supervision of a bean-counter manager and eventually one or the other is out the door. Testing can help you spot these potential teamwork issues and provide valuable intelligence for assigning the right kind of rep to the right type of manager. It's important to match the needs and skills of people to the right sales and management environment.

Objection #1—"I'm worried about the liability of giving selection tests."

It's a sign of the times. J. C. Penney didn't worry about government guidelines for hiring and firing. But today legal issues have become the number-one concern among HR professionals and sales recruiters. Liability issues are more top of mind for potential test users than cost or need. As overburdened as business owners and managers feel with government regulations and requirements, US law is still relatively lenient compared to legal requirements in parts of Europe, Australia, or New Zealand, where it usually takes a full year or longer for companies to document a dismissal for any reason.

Managers and recruiters frequently ask, "How do I know if the assessment I use is approved by the EEOC?" There are no government-approved selection tests. The EEOC does not endorse any test. The law requires that selection tests must do two simple things: they must measure something critical to job performance, and they must not discriminate on any grounds other than variables associated with job performance. Hiring tests are, by definition, discriminatory; that is, they classify individuals according to some variable. As long as recruiters can document that the discriminating variable being assessed is critical to job performance, Hire Performers have nothing to fear from government regulators.

Tom, for instance, was a sales recruiter from a small manufacturing company. He used a well-known sales-personality test to screen candidates but was also interested in our assessment. "We've been using this assessment for years," Tom said. "Why should I use yours? Aren't all these hiring tests the same?" Barnett asked Tom if he could look at the job description for the position he was trying to fill. It only took a second or two to see that Tom's company could be legally vulnerable.

"What does that personality test tell you about your candidates?" Barnett asked Tom. "What are you looking for?"

"Drive, determination, somebody really outgoing—the usual stuff," he replied.

"Where is that stuff in your job description?" Barnett asked, handing him the job description. It wasn't there. His job description was a list of behaviors—what Tom expected salespeople to do, not what they should be. The salesperson who sold Tom the personality test claimed that drive, determination, and extroversion were important for salespeople. Tom couldn't disagree, but without specifically stating that these attributes were required, any applicant turned down on the basis of the profile could sue Tom's company and had a very good chance of winning.

All the parts of Hire Performance work together synergistically. When approached strategically, the ad will work with the assessment;

the assessment will dovetail with the interview; and the interview will jibe with motivational strategy. Each contributes to all the others and reinforces the goal of recruiting a winning sales team.

But even if Tom includes those psychological buzzwords in the job description, the company is still exposed. All that is required is for some troublemaker to make Tom produce his turnover statistics and ask for the reasons of dismissal. Since everybody took the same hiring profile, it's obvious that a lot of people who tested high in drive, determination, or extroversion turned out to be job failures. Tom was inferring a connection between production and personality that just isn't there. And quick as a flash, your attorney is whispering in your ear, "We'd better settle."

When Dr. Barnett was first designing SalesKey, one manager who had grown cynical about using selection assessments asked, "If these tests are so #@&%$ good at predicting behavior, why can't they spot the people who are most likely to sue me if they don't like the results?" At first he dismissed the objection as just one more manager having a bad day. But after considerable thought, this idea began to make sense. Barnett came up with something he called Validity Check.

The SalesKey Validity Check scale actually has nothing to do with statistical validity. It is designed to provoke and measure behaviors that indicate how open the test taker may or may not be to getting objective feedback about results. Not everyone who takes a hiring test is happy about it. SalesKey detects and measures this attitude toward taking the assessment. If the test taker gets upset while completing the questionnaire, the Validity Check score drops. When it reaches a certain point, it tells the defensive test taker to ignore the results because the data is unreliable. Are the scores really unreliable? Not at all. The assessment has a built-in safeguard to help reduce the risk of someone becoming upset by test results and taking it out on you or your sales organization.

Make sure that any sales test you are using measures what is actually important to the job.

TWO KINDS OF TESTS

Sales-hiring tests can be divided into two general classifications: sales-personality tests and behavioral profiles (sometimes called competency tests). As stated earlier, sales-personality tests are the most popular type of sales assessment. They've been around a long time. Sales-personality tests attempt to measure the psychological makeup of the individual, peering deep inside the candidate's character and inborn traits. The assumption behind personality profiling is that it takes a certain kind of person to succeed in sales; a person usually described with words like "extroverted," "social," "outgoing"; someone possessing "ego strength" and "drive." Sales-personality tests assume that if someone possesses the right stuff, she will be comfortable meeting people and promoting the company's product or service. Identifying a sales-personality test can be difficult, because the assessment may not use the word "personality" in its title or description. Sometimes they're called temperament or preference profiles. One easy way to spot a sales-personality assessment is to look at what is being measured. Do the scales (the characteristics being measured) describe an objective behavior or an abstract mental state? What about words like strong-minded, dominance, optimistic, amiable, steady, and competent? If these are behaviors, then we should be able to objectively say whether or not a person is doing something. What does someone *do* to be strong-minded? Is optimism a behavior or a cognitive state? If it's an objective behavior, we should be able to say without argument that candidate X is more competent than candidate Y. But optimism could lie in the eye of the beholder. We're not saying you can't assess for these things. We are saying that these personality characteristics are *inferred* from behavior and are not the behavior itself.

The second type of sales-hiring test measures behaviors. They attempt to measure the basic skills necessary for the job. Behavioral profiles don't look behind the mental-motivation curtain at all. Behavior tests are only interested in what people do, what is purely observable and external. Does applicant A or applicant B have more experience doing a specific skill? Who types faster? Who has a certification and who doesn't?

The behavioral-competency tests can be just as problematic as personality tests. They are worthless for recruiting entry-level salespeople. If your candidate has no experience in sales, there's not much point in asking a lot about sales-specific behaviors. One good predictor of sales success in any sales organization is tenure. The longer someone is in a position, the more likely he or she is to sell more. But every top producer started out as an inexperienced rookie whom someone took a risk to hire. Maybe they used a sales-personality test. Even broken clocks are right twice a day.

But the greater problem with behavioral-competency tests is that they reduce flesh-and-blood people to impersonal statistics. This is great for analyzer recruiters who are looking for the silver bullet to make an impersonal decision on a statistical basis. But the fact is that people are more than their behaviors. When you see someone crying, you don't think, "Oh, that person is secreting a saline solution." You wonder what's wrong; how is the person hurting? Purely behavioral assessments are going to be useless when it comes to developing sales talent, because selling is so complex. It isn't just one or ten behaviors but hundreds. As long as imperfect people are making the decisions about whom to hire, there is going to be error and inefficiency. No assessment is 100 percent perfect. That's because they were developed by humans and are completed by humans. Believe it or not, people don't always tell the truth on assessments. They may not understand a question but answer it anyway, or they interpret a word differently than what the test designer had in mind. And what possesses some people to try to sabotage their own assessment results is beyond us. There are many reasons why we can't treat people like machines. People are not completely predictable, because individuals are more than the sum of their behaviors.

This is why Barnett developed SalesKey to measure behaviors, aptitudes, skills, job preferences, and even personality, because the research said they all impact sales productivity. It is a combination of both types of assessments. We feel that the best sales assessments are those that can continue to deliver value after the hiring decision. The biggest difference between SalesKey and other assessments is that it is a developmental portrait of the rep regardless if he or she is a veteran or a rookie.

WHAT SALES-HIRING TEST SHOULD I USE?

Here are some things to look for in an assessment that will make you a smarter consumer of sales-hiring tests.

IS IT STREET LEGAL?

In 2009 the US Supreme Court heard the case of *Ricci v. DeStefano*, better known as the "New Haven firefighter's lawsuit." The details of this case were widely reported in the media; however, there was little focus on how the Supreme Court's decision will affect the use of personnel-selection assessments.

Ricci v. DeStefano began when the city of New Haven used a test in order to determine eligibility for promoting firefighters to the rank of captain and lieutenant. It turned out that African American and Hispanic applicants obtained lower test scores, and none was eligible for promotion. City officials decided to abandon the test results and refused to certify any successful candidates for promotion. The white firefighters then sued the city in order to make the test results stand. Many experts in selection assessments reviewed the test used in New Haven and found serious, indeed fatal, problems with it. Even though the Supreme Court eventually ruled in favor of the white firefighters, three important criteria were established for any assessment used in determining job eligibility.

1. *The test must be well constructed.*
   Assessments need to document a process by which they were created. That process involves the following:
   - a job analysis describing the tasks or activities, the working conditions, schedules, and possible hazards associated with the work
   - identification of relevant success metrics; that is, how is success evaluated
   - identification of the knowledge, skills, abilities, and other individual characteristics necessary to complete the job
   - development of an instrument to measure those KSAOs

2. *The test must be empirically validated.*

    Statistical studies need to validate that what the test is measuring is related to job performance. Specifically, the process calls for determining the strength of the correlations between test scales and the success metrics. In other words, do the people who score high on the assessment's measurements of KSAOs actually sell more?

3. *The test must not unfairly discriminate.*

    US law creates certain protected classes of individuals. Tests cannot favor one group of people more than another. This was the problem that brought the New Haven firefighters to the Supreme Court. Ask for the technical manual of the sales assessment you are considering. Look for the adverse impact studies to be sure the assessment is EEOC compliant. This study needs to be done only once in order for the test to be validated. You do not need to repeat it for your company.

IS IT PREDICTIVE?

Don't settle for sales stories or be impressed with client lists. Ask for the technical manual for the assessment and read it. This publication can be quite confusing if you're not an academic. Some companies actually take advantage of the statistics phobia of most sales managers and recruiters. Most assessments publish their reliability data, not their predictive-validity data. A test's reliability is whether it gives the same results across multiple administrations; that is, if I take it today and it says my score is 90 and I take it a week from now and my score is a 40, the assessment may not be reliable. There are two common measures of reliability: test-retest and something called Cronbach's alpha. You don't need to know what all that is unless you want to study the subject further. But those statistics aren't going to tell you if the assessment predicts performance.

Another trick of technical manuals to confuse the consumer is to publish validation statistics that still have nothing to do with predictive validity. That's because there are four major types of validity.

- Face validity means the questions appear to be at least superficially related to the subject under study.
- Content validity means subject-matter experts have reviewed the appropriateness of questions to measure a specific trait.
- Construct validity is getting closer to what you need to know. It measures whether the questionnaire actually measures what it purports to measure; in other words, do people who score high on energy actually have more energy? But this is still not the same as predictive validity (sometimes called concurrent validity). The first three types of validation are concerned with the questionnaire.
- Predictive validity is concerned with results in the real world. Are there statistically significant correlations between test scores and production metrics? Only SalesKey and one other sales assessment publish predictive-validation statistics.

If your company has 100 people or more, you should probably carry out your own predictive-validity study. Give the assessment to your salespeople, collect your success metrics, and see if there are any correlations. If there aren't, it doesn't automatically mean that the assessment is flawed. It usually means that there is "noise" in the data, which, simplistically speaking, means that you're trying to compare apples and oranges. You want to be sure that what the assessment is measuring is roughly the same thing as you are counting as a success metric.

In more than fifty corporate predictive-validity studies, SalesKey has correlated with metrics of successful salespeople after correcting the data for tenure. Many times companies give us sales volume as a success metric against which to compare test scores. We sometimes find that there is no correlation between what SalesKey measures and the metrics provided. But frequently we discover that's because there is no correlation between activities and sales volume in the organization. Managers give reps accounts. Veterans cherry-pick larger-volume sales. If the publisher of the assessment cannot answer your questions satisfactorily, ask a psychology or statistics professor at a local college for help in setting up these kinds of studies to be certain you're getting an accurate picture of what an assessment can and cannot do.

ESTABLISH A BENCHMARK

Once you've discovered correlations that demonstrate that the assessment is predicting your success metrics, you're ready to establish your selection benchmarks. You want to know what differentiates top producers from the also-rans. Invariably, we run across companies that want us to test their top producers and construct an ideal-employee typology against which they may evaluate candidates. This is called person-environmental fit theory. There are a number of problems with this widely practiced approach to validation and selection.

1. What information is used to evaluate sales talent? The more subjective the evaluation used, the less reliable will be the results. In one of our studies, we discovered that a company's top producers were differentiated by high coachability and low control needs. The success metric used in the study was a ranking done by the rep's managers. It was obvious that these managers were rating most highly the salespeople who were compliant and not likely to cause trouble. Managerial rankings are subjective and in our experience may not conform to actual productivity. But even using more objective production data can be skewed by latent variables (e.g., managers giving favored employees more lucrative regions, etc.).

2. The ideal employee scenario that tests only top producers reduces the sample size. The statistical methods used to construct a hiring template work best with large sample sizes. For example, one can create a regression formula with twenty or thirty people, but these formulae rarely work in the real world. You can't do good statistics working with only the outliers. You need data that is going to look more like the population of the people who walk in your door to apply for a job.

3. Person-environment fit theory may overlook the attributes of bottom producers. What if the worst salespeople also score within the same range on those critical scales as reps judged to be the best? If you really want to know what differentiates top and bottom salespeople, you have to test both and then use the appropriate statistical method to find the variables that differentiate them. But let's say you've included poor salespeople along with top reps in your study, and the typology of top producers is unique to your most productive salespeople. Limiting your search to these attributes undermines any improvement in your company's sales strategy, tactics, or techniques. The typology assumes that there is only one best way to sell at your company and your current crop of stars has mastered it. And consider this: how can you be sure your top producers really are top-performing salespeople? One company's top guns might be quite mediocre at a competitor. By only looking at salespeople in one company, users of the typology approach guarantee the status quo.

4. Still another problem with the typology approach: it leaves no room for training or development. Comparing candidates to an ideal salesperson based on your top producers provides little information or incentive for coaching, developing, and retaining sales talent.

5. Finally, it's so easy to disprove the typology approach. Just look at turnover or the high number of candidates scoring well on a typology-driven assessment. If these new hires don't in fact become top producers, then the model will have been proven to be false. Or, taken to the other extreme, if 50 percent of your candidates meet the typology based on your top 10–15 percent of salespeople, the model will have been discredited.

SalesKey benchmarking uses only large sample sizes and includes a sample of as many salespeople in a company as possible, not just top performers. The benchmark is not foolproof, but any good validation study should be able to tell you how often the formula should work.

CONCLUSION

Be a smart consumer of sales-selection tests. Be clear about what you expect an assessment to do and read the technical manual to determine if the test meets the stringent requirements for both being street legal and predictive. If possible, do your own predictive validity study to help establish accurate benchmarks for recruiting.

19

DEBRIEFING TEST RESULTS

The purpose of your first interview was to get a general picture of the applicant's experience, self-presentation, social skills, and potential fit within the organization. The second interview is designed to gather more in-depth information about qualifications, skills, and possible productivity issues. Using a sales-hiring test should provide you with objective information about specific productivity issues the applicant may bring to the job, issues that you need to confirm, deny, and evaluate.

Review the assessment report for strengths and challenges. What are the positives and negatives the instrument identifies? Do they correspond to your review of the résumé? Prior to the interview, get out the colored markers you used to highlight the candidate's résumé and use the same color scheme to review test results. After the interview, ask yourself, "Did the candidate correspond to the behaviors I saw in the interview?" If the assessment highlights significant issues you saw in action during the interview, it's a pretty good sign that you are not headed in a good direction.

SHARING ASSESSMENT RESULTS

Although many recruiters will never need to develop this Level 4 skill because they don't discuss assessment results, in some cases the hiring manager might want to review results with the applicant. In several European countries, if an employer provides an assessment, the recruiter is expected to review the results with the individual. We think that trend is likely to continue and take hold in this country as well. So here are some ideas about sharing assessment results.

KEEP IT GENERAL

Sales-hiring tests can provide you with valuable information for the second interview. Results can and should be used without necessarily investing the time to go over the meaning of every scale and how the applicant scored. If the recruiter is also going to be the candidate's manager and the candidate has positive test results, using this information can forge a strong bond between the interviewer and the applicant. Top producers are always open to learning anything about themselves that will improve their productivity. Potential superstars will appreciate your taking time to give them professional feedback. It demonstrates a powerful commitment on your part to develop their sales potential. On the other hand, poor results should probably not be shared with test takers. You're not running a testing service. If an applicant wants to know how he or she did on the test, always make these specific points:

1. It's not a test, because there is no right or wrong answers to pass or to fail.
2. We use the questionnaire to determine your skill level and possible fit to the position.
3. The questionnaire is only one source of information we use to make a hiring decision.

We recommend that you quickly summarize one or two strengths and move on with the interview. We do not recommend cutoff scores (above this number, hire; below that number, don't hire) because it violates our recruitment strategy statement, making people subservient to things. Blaming the test as the reason you did not hire a candidate could leave you open to legal hassles if the test you use is not properly researched and validated. Selection assessments may supplement Hire Performance but are never a substitute for the recruiter's professionalism and responsibility.

DON'T CALL IT A TEST

"Test" implies there are right and wrong answers. To most people, "test" means pass or fail. Get in the habit of referring to it as a questionnaire or a survey. This helps demystify the instrument and any findings. Assessments aren't perfect. They make mistakes. People make mistakes in how they answer. The hiring "test" is really a tool to help you ask better questions from which to make a profitable decision for both the company and the applicant.

USE YOUR OWN PROFILE

Have your own profile ready to share with candidates. Show the candidate how you were rated by the assessment. Do this first before revealing the applicant's report. This allows you to talk about what the tool measures in a way less threatening to the candidate. If you are self-revealing about your profile, you will not only diminish any sense of threat but can also build a powerful bond between you and the applicant. This technique is especially effective if the candidate is challenged in a way that matches your profile. Rather than feeling emotionally threatened by this information, you use assessment insights proactively to underscore your commitment to be a sales coach and not merely a babysitter.

MIRROR THE APPLICANT'S RESPONSE

Some recruiters are uncertain how to introduce assessment results into the interview. The simplest approach is probably the best. Ask the candidate, "How did you feel about taking the survey?" Listen carefully to whatever emotion may be lurking behind the words as the applicant responds. Is he apprehensive? Is she curious? Did he feel threatened? Is the individual dismissive? Is she open to learning anything she can about herself? Is this salesperson coachable? What does the reaction to the assessment say about emotional maturity? Whatever the reaction, reflect those emotions back to the applicant. Mirroring is not mimicking. You are reflecting back the emotional feelings behind the words as well as listening and reacting to what they say. Your applicant acts concerned, for example. Reflect her apprehension by saying, "You know, I had some of those same feelings when I first took that questionnaire. Here's what it said about me." Then pull out your assessment results. If the candidate is dismissive of the test as "no big deal," mirror his dismissive attitude by saying, "Yeah, I didn't think you'd have any trouble with that." Mirroring keeps you on the same side of the issue as the candidate. The worst reaction is to become defensive about using the sales test. Invariably this calls attention to the transactional nature of the test rather than its strategic importance to your interview. The issue isn't what the individual scored but what the scores say about his or her fit within your sales culture. Becoming defensive puts the assessment instead of your professional evaluation at center stage.

CQ

This is a simple technique for handling what might be perceived as critical or uncomplimentary information in the hiring interview. CQ stands for "compliment then question." Never voice a concern or ask a potentially difficult question that you haven't prefaced with a strength found in the candidate's skills and qualifications. CQ can help minimize defensive reactions and help candidates feel more at ease with you. Since you don't want to be fumbling for a compliment during the interview, jot down some compliments next to the areas of concern on the assessment report or the in the margins of the résumé and circle them in blue (blue indicates strengths). As the interview proceeds, always CQ; keep that same 1:1 ratio of compliment to a question. You may not intend for a statement to be critical, but some applicants may perceive anything less than complimentary as a critique, especially sensitive empathizers. If an applicant doesn't seem able or ready to talk about a particular subject, move to another complementary topic before reopening the matter of concern.

When you raise issues that could impact productivity, try to avoid making pronouncements. Always pose your concerns as questions. Depending on the overall quality of the candidate, highlight one or two of the main issues. (If you are using our SalesKey Behavioral Interview Summary, the top three issues will be identified for you along with behavioral-interview questions to ask based on the applicant's scores.) Don't blame the test by saying, "You scored low on risk sensitivity." Frame your discussion of risk sensitivity around an open-ended question that describes the behavior. For example, you could discuss a low risk-sensitivity score by saying, "You answered some questions in such a way as to indicate you might like to live a little dangerously from time to time. Does that sound like you?" Or perhaps you have a concern about the individual's sales identity. Instead of saying, "Your sales-identity score was low," CQ: "Your profile showed that you have a lot of initiative. Some of your answers on the questionnaire indicate that you may not want to be associated with some aspects of being a salesperson. Would you agree or disagree with that opinion?" Assessment scores are just numbers; test results are not facts; they are estimates of the individual's behaviors and aptitudes. You should treat any assessment's results as hypotheses that require further investigation.

LET THE CANDIDATE TALK ABOUT THE RESULTS

Do some of the issues you raise appear to be more acceptable to the applicant than others? What results seem to cause questions or concern? It's important that you not become defensive about having given the assessment or reporting its conclusions. Performers will dismiss problem areas with a wave of the hand and a funny remark. Controllers will argue and disagree with almost anything that is less than positive. Analyzers tend to grow quiet and carefully weigh their answers before responding. Empathizers tend to give "yes ... but" responses, agreeing with you on the surface and at the same time mollifying your concern with a smile and assurance that the issue is no longer a problem. The purpose of giving any hiring test should never be to label or categorize people but to encourage candidates to talk about issues important to sales productivity.

TAKE A BREAK

Immediately after concluding your review of results, excuse yourself from the room. Go to the restroom, get a cup of coffee, go talk with your assistant—anything to give the candidate a few moments to integrate the information you've just shared. Additionally, the break provides space and time to distance yourself from the role of coach and reestablish your role as interviewer with the candidate.

CONCLUSION

Reviewing an applicant's hiring test results can be a positive step if the candidate's profile is good and the recruiter wants to build a powerful bond with the potential sales superstar. Several best practices about debriefing assessment results include:

- Avoid calling it a test.
- Use your own test results to debrief someone anxious about performance.
- Always compliment before raising a concern.
- Always pose concerns as open-ended questions.
- Encourage the applicant to talk about what he or she has learned.
- Take a break after reviewing results to let the applicant think about the information presented.

20

BEHAVIORAL INTERVIEWING

Formulating your hypotheses about candidates doesn't have to be complicated. Testing your hypotheses shouldn't be difficult. Hire Performance is about reading behaviors to infer sales productivity. If John's record from the Department of Motor Vehicles is as long as your arm, your hypothesis will probably be that John is reckless and takes unnecessary risks. If Kim shakes hands limply and talks softly, your hypothesis may be that she may have trouble initiating contact and assertively closing sales. Behaviors help us form hypotheses. Then we are going to test those hypotheses by using a Level 4 skill called *behavioral interviewing.*

THE THREE MOST DANGEROUS CATEGORIES
OF INTERVIEW QUESTIONS

Behavioral interviewing is a method of asking objective, behaviorally relevant questions about past performance in order to help recruiters predict future behavior. Behavioral interviewing is a skill that, if practiced carefully and methodically, should help you avoid the three most dangerous and counterproductive categories of interview questions:

1.   Illegal questions
2.   Hypothetical questions
3.   Feeling-oriented questions

1. ILLEGAL QUESTIONS

Here are some illegal questions to avoid and permissible alternatives that you may ask in the hiring situation.

Questions about national citizenship or ethnic origin
 Illegal   "Are you an American citizen?"
 Legal   "Are you authorized to work in the United States?"
      "What languages do you read or write?"
      Note: This question is illegal unless being bilingual is critical to performing the job.

Questions about age
 Illegal   "How old are you?"
      "When did you graduate from high school (or college)?"
      "What is your birth date?"
 Legal   "Are you over eighteen years of age?"

Questions about marital or family status
 Illegal   "Are you married?"
      "With whom do you reside?"
      "Do you plan to have a family?"
      "How many children do you have?"
      "What are your childcare arrangements?"
 Legal   "Are you willing to relocate if necessary?"
      "Are you free to travel?"
      "The work requires considerable overtime. Can you work overtime as needed?"
      Note: These questions are legal only if asked of *all* candidates being considered for the position.

Personal questions
Illegal   "How much do you weigh?"
                  "How tall are you?"
                  "When was the date of your last physical?"
Legal   "Are you able to lift fifty pounds and carry it one
                  hundred feet, as this is critical to the job?"
                  Note: These questions are legal only if asked of *all*
                  candidates being considered for the position.

Questions about disabilities
Illegal   "Do you have any disabilities?"
                  Asking about details of any obvious disability
                  ("How did you lose your arm?")
Legal   "Are you able to perform the physical duties of
                  this job?"
                  Note: This question is legal only if asked after
                  describing the physical requirements of the
                  job and if asked equally of *all* candidates being
                  considered for the position.

Questions about criminal background
Illegal   "Have you ever been arrested?"
Legal   "Have you ever been arrested for _____?"
                  Note: This question is legal only if asked about a
                  crime reasonably related to the job and if asked
                  equally of *all* candidates being considered for
                  the position.

It is against US law to ask any questions about religion, race or
ethnic background, national origin, gender, age, marital or family status,
sexual orientation, physical disability, arrests, or financial status. Best
rule of thumb: if it's personal, don't ask. If a candidate volunteers any
prohibited information, inform the candidate that you appreciate their
openness but you will not make any hiring decision on any basis other
than the skills and qualifications of candidates.

2. HYPOTHETICAL QUESTIONS

Hypothetical questions are not illegal, but they are counterproductive because they don't reveal anything except the candidate's creative abilities. Avoid asking "What if …" questions. One of the most common mistakes made by recruiters is using hypothetical scenario questions. For example, avoid asking, "How would you handle this or that situation?" Behavioral interviewing roots a question to a specific point in time. Ask, "Tell me about a time you did such and so," or, "On your last job, how did you handle this situation?"

The best recruiters invariably say that the best predictor of future performance is past performance. If a candidate has not faced the situation you describe, you are more likely to find out the truth by asking behavioral questions than hypothetical ones.

3. FEELING-ORIENTED QUESTIONS

Any question that begins "How do you feel about …" moves you in the wrong direction if your goal is to build a winning sales team. Hire Performance is fact driven, not feeling oriented. You're not hiring the candidate to feel anything but to do something. Just because a candidate reports certain feelings toward a subject doesn't necessarily mean that your rep will behave in ways consistent with those feelings. Feelings are fleeting and transitory. Behavior is objective. Don't confuse emotional needs with feelings. Emotional needs are the root causes of behavior. Feelings are usually the mental subjective feedback of behavior. We infer emotional needs from specific behavior.

HIRE PERFORMANCE BEHAVIORAL-INTERVIEWING GUIDE

The second interview must uncover and address potential and actual problem areas in your candidate's background and present situations that could impact productivity. But what do you ask? This section helps take the guesswork out of constructing a great interview. Here are the issues you need to explore in order of their impact on productivity. (Of course, if you use SalesKey these and many more questions are provided for you in the behavioral-interview report.) For each behavior, we'll suggest some behavioral-interview questions and outline how you might interpret candidate responses.

ENERGY

Definition: Career energy is the amount of physical stamina the candidate brings to a sales career. Selling is physically demanding, particularly for outside salespeople who must travel from place to place. People who sell primarily on the phone should have above-average stamina, but not too much. Inside salespeople with high levels of energy may grow restless in a sedentary position. Low-energy individuals start more tasks than they finish. Successful salespeople get proper rest and have a balanced lifestyle. Top producers tend to be more energetic.

How to Spot the Problem:
Career energy can be difficult to spot in a typical employment interview. Candidates are usually well prepared and eager to make a positive impression. Energy issues don't generally show up until after the person experiences the daily grind of the job. But there are some ways to spot energy problems in the interview. There are some obvious indicators of energy-management issues: Does the candidate seem listless? Do you catch the candidate suppressing yawns? Does the résumé contain obvious typographical errors? If so, your candidate may suffer from low energy. Fidgeting, finger tapping, and knee bouncing are signs of nervous energy that may or may not be applicable to the energy required to do the job.

Hobbies are another indicator of energy level. People who relax with strenuous activity (jogging, biking, team sports) tend to possess higher levels of energy than individuals with passive hobbies (reading, movies, collecting things, etc.). People with high levels of energy miss fewer days due to illness and are less likely to be overweight or visibly underweight. Here are some specific behavioral-interview questions to address the energy issue.

| Question: | "Tell me about a time in your career when you had to give it 110 percent. What was it and how did you specifically go beyond what was expected of you?" |

| Interpretation: | Can the candidate provide an example?
What represents "110 percent" to the candidate? Is it enough for your company?
What was the event? Is it transferable to your business?
Watch body language and listen for excuses. |

| Question: | "Our most successful reps work long hours. It's not unusual to put in sixty to seventy hours per week. What's the typical work week where you worked before?" |

| Interpretation: | Watch the candidate's expression when you mention the amount of long hours. Can you detect any element of surprise? (You may have to be especially alert to nonverbal clues like small eye and mouth movements.) Does the candidate shift in his chair? These are indicators of stress. Low-energy individuals often sigh when they talk about working long hours, or they may express displeasure in other passive ways. High-energy individuals will not make a big deal of the issue, although some may forcefully attack the practice of their former employer as being unnecessary or a function of poor management. Don't be as distracted by what the candidate says about working long hours as how they say it. High-energy individuals are quick and direct, while reps with lower energy tend to be slower at tasks and indirect with responses.
Without a history of heavy workloads, it's very likely this individual will not put in the hours required to succeed if you have determined that your top reps must work more than the typical forty-hour week. |

GOAL ORIENTATION

Definition: Goal orientation measures the ability of the individual to set performance goals and work toward achieving them on a regular basis. Hire Performance is driven by objective data. Top performers know on any given day where they stand in relation to their goals—how many calls they need to make, how many appointments will yield opportunities to close sales that will meet and exceed quota. Poor performers are more likely to measure performance subjectively on the basis of feelings rather than by preplanned, objective measures of success. High-goal-orientation reps will know where they are going in their career and will likely have a timetable for achieving their strategic objectives. Low-goal-orientation reps tend to watch things happen rather than make things happen.

How to Spot the Problem:

Like career energy, goal-orientation issues seldom manifest themselves in the typical employment interview. Candidates will be prepared for the often-used hypothetical question like "Where do you see yourself in five years?" We said previously that this question can be used as a kind of ice breaker, but it's not likely to yield a lot of specific information. Recruiters often mistake candidate enthusiasm for goal orientation. Emotional measures of performance undermine the motivating power of goals.

One simple behavioral measure of goal orientation is whether the candidate was on time for the interview. Strongly goal-oriented people will show up early. They come prepared with questions, particularly questions about the company's goals. Another window on the applicant's goal orientation is opened when you ask about performance standards at her last job. Did the rep have quotas? Were they enforced, or like some motivational poster, were they used for decorative purposes only? Can the candidate identify the success ratios necessary to meet performance measures? If not, goal-orientation behaviors were probably not internalized because they weren't all that meaningful either to the company or to the candidate. In either case, it could indicate someone with emotional measures of success rather than a truly goal-oriented salesperson. Here are some samples of goal orientation behavioral-interview questions.

Question:	"What percentage of your sales calls result in presentations and sales?" Or "What was/is your close ratio?"
Interpretation:	If the candidate has experience in sales, does the applicant know his or her close ratio? How does this salesperson's experience fit with the ratios for your own product/service? Watch body language and listen for feeling-oriented ways of measuring success rather than objective measurements.
Question:	"How do you know when you've done a good job?"
Interpretation:	The more a candidate struggles with the answer to this question, the lower the goal orientation. If goals aren't clearly defined, the salesperson may never really know when they've done a good job, because they are relying on subjective definitions of job satisfaction. Listen for emotional measures vs. objective measures of success. Low-goal-orientation individuals use feelings to measure success, while candidates with sufficient goal orientation refer to the number of sales made, percent of incremental sales, number of months above quota, dollars generated—number, numbers, numbers. Highly goal-oriented individuals with no previous sales experience should also measure success in the attainment of objectives rather than acquiring feelings. This question will also quickly uncover selling style and unbalanced life needs. The approval-driven empathizer is likely to talk about getting positive feedback from the manager or others on the team. The

empathizer measures success by the praise of people he knows. The attention-seeking performers may boast about prizes won and other forms of personal and professional recognition. The information-starved analyzer may go a little overboard on the numbers, while the controller may discount the motivating power of anything and everything outside him or herself.

Question: "What are your income goals for the next twelve and twenty-four months?"

Interpretation: Do these goals match the income you require in order for you to count your salesperson a success? If a candidate only expects to make $35,000 in twelve months and you know that in order for this person to be a productive rep she will need to make $50,000, it may indicate insufficient goal orientation. Of course, she will say she wants to earn $50,000, but if her internal gauge is set at $35,000, she may get comfortable with an effort sufficient to keep her job but not excel.

If the individual's earning expectations are completely out of line with the reality of the position you are offering, you will need to drill down deeper on the financial needs of the individual. If the income expectations are reasonable given his most recent position or in line with new training received, then you will need to address the situation directly. Your position may not be enough to inspire effort and satisfy the candidate's needs. Even if you were able to hire him for less money, chances are that he will stay only until he finds another position paying the money he wants.

SALES IDENTITY

Definition: Sales identity is the degree of pride one takes in being a salesperson. People with low sales identity are quick to believe negative stereotypes about salespeople. Reps that spend lots of money on motivational tapes and books may have an addiction to "feel good" solutions that momentarily counteract their negative feelings but that eventually create cynicism and burnout. Over half of salespeople with poor sales identity are not even aware of this career-threatening condition. Most candidates will credit their poor attitude toward sales to a bad previous experience they believe will be overcome in the new job. Of course, sometimes that's true. But in many cases it's a self-fulfilling prophecy of someone who brings a subconscious bias against salespeople to the job.

How to Spot the Problem:
Examine your candidate's résumé. Look at the job titles previously held. If a previous employer referred to a sales position as "Account Manager," "Relationship Consultant," or some other swapped-out sales identity, you'll want to be sure the rep didn't come away from the job with a negative sales identity. Ask these questions.

Question: (If résumé shows other titles for the sales function) "I see at your last job you were called … (fill in the title). Was this a sales job? Why do you think the company used another title for 'salesperson'?"

Interpretation: Does your candidate talk about avoiding the negative stereotypes associated with salespeople? If so, assume your candidate may have some residual sales-identity issues.
Does the candidate explain that the title helped salespeople sell more or in some other way improved initiative, or was the phony designation used as an excuse or apology?
Watch body language and listen for any negative image of salespeople.

Question: "What do you need in a sales manager? How important is it for a sales manager to help salespeople feel good about what they do?"

Interpretation: Does the candidate say that it's important for managers to help salespeople feel good about being in sales? If so, this could indicate a negative view toward selling or someone who does not value a sales career.

What behaviors does the candidate say are necessary management behaviors? Are manager behaviors accountability oriented (coach top performance) or motivation oriented (keep the rep feeling good)? Motivational themes may indicate poor sales identity (particularly if combined with poor sales initiative).

Do you hear an overreliance on clichés and motivational responses that provide shallow and superficial answers to complex problems? This is a strong indication of someone who has not thought through the daily grind of selling.

Watch body language and listen for a negative image of salespeople.

OUT-OF-BALANCE RISK SENSITIVITY

Definition: Risk sensitivity is the degree to which an individual is comfortable taking legitimate risks. Salespeople need a balanced risk sensitivity—too little and a rep could take unnecessary risks and not do "due diligence"; too much and your candidate may be paralyzed by worry about worst-case scenarios. People with high risk sensitivity will have difficulty selling any product or service that involves risk to the consumer. These worrywarts do not manage stress well and are easily overwhelmed with deadlines and pressure. Research shows that high risk sensitivity can be catastrophic to sales productivity in direct-sales organizations due to a view of prospecting as risky behavior socially if not physically. Low risk sensitivity cannot be tolerated in sales organizations that are highly regulated or require a great deal of care or precision (technical sales, pharmaceutical sales, etc.).

How to Spot the Problem:
As we stated in a previous chapter, hobbies are frequently a reliable behavioral clue to risk sensitivity. If hobbies are not included on the résumé, ask about them in the interview. But another aspect of people with risk sensitivity issues is that they frequently do not do well in crisis situations. When the environment suddenly becomes unpredictable, the need for stability can be overwhelming in some people. If the candidate was late for the interview, was he overwhelmed with anxiety? Did she seem overly flustered, profusely apologizing and struggling to regain composure? People with unbalanced risk sensitivity do not handle stress well. They may appear nervous in the interview. Consider these questions.

Question: "Tell me about a time in your career when you faced a crisis. What did you do to weather it?"

Interpretation: Is the candidate quick or slow to respond? Does the candidate's description of crisis seem appropriate?
Low-risk-sensitive candidates may have difficulty remembering a single instance. High-risk-sensitive candidates may have difficulty limiting their answer to one instance.
Watch body language and listen for signals of someone who doesn't work well under pressure or who may take unnecessary risks.

Question: "This job can become highly stressful at times. What are some specific ways you've learned to manage stress?"

Interpretation: Is the candidate quick or slow to respond? Is the applicant able to describe a stress-management strategy? High-risk-sensitivity individuals become uncomfortable talking about the subject. You will see it in their avoidance of the question and in their closed body language. High-risk-sensitivity candidates could have a detailed answer, as they experience stress quite frequently.

Low-risk-sensitivity candidates (risk takers) are more likely to discount stress problems. They believe that they work best under pressure. Watch body language and listen for signals of someone who has an out-of-balance risk sensitivity.

Question: "What is your preferred method of compensation? Do you prefer a high salary with a limited upside or a lower salary and unlimited income potential based on performance?"

Interpretation: High-risk-sensitive individuals will prefer their compensation package to be more strongly guaranteed than someone who is comfortable taking risks. You also want to be sure there is a fit between your organization's comp plan and the preferences of your candidate. This Level 1 attribute is very difficult to modify in people, so to prevent costly turnover, be sure your pay meets their emotional needs and expectations.

SALES INITIATIVE

Definition: Sales initiative is the inclination of the salesperson to make contacts rather than excuses. Reluctant to make calls, candidates with low sales initiative are likely to place certain types of people off-limits to prospecting or hesitate to use all available means for gaining entrance to new or existing business relationships.

How to Spot the Problem:
A sales-initiative problem is almost impossible to spot without the help of a sales assessment designed to measure it. In job interviews,

candidates appear almost superhuman; nothing is too difficult or will stand in their way of succeeding. It's like fire walking at one of those motivational seminars; almost anyone can generate enough courage and bravado to scamper across the hot coals, once, to the cheers of comrades. The trouble with selling is that it is so every day and often so solitary. Refusals and rebuffs wear thin on many reps, and they'll quickly develop excuses for avoiding the rejection.

One way to gauge sales initiative is to keep track of candidates who follow up their résumé with a phone call or some other form of contact. Did your applicant phone ahead to confirm your interview? Did the candidate send you a thank-you note or e-mail after the first interview? These behaviors could indicate strong sales initiative.

Perhaps the best way to measure sales initiative is to build it into your interview process. If you can afford to be highly selective, only do second interviews with candidates who recontact you. This may be the most reliable test for candidates with no previous sales experience. They are, after all, attempting to sell themselves to you as a recruiter. Applicants who sit and wait for the phone to ring are likely to exhibit the same behavior on your payroll. Here are some sample questions for behavioral interviewing to the initiative issue.

Question: "How did you generate new business in your last sales position?"

Interpretation: Is the candidate quick or slow to respond? Does the candidate's business-generation model contradict or complement your own?
                  Were leads provided in the applicant's last sales job? If so, what attitudes toward prospecting did this practice create and reinforce? Salespeople with low sales initiative tend to view prospecting as unprofessional or as a necessary evil, something they can stop when they succeed.
                  Watch body language and listen for any built-in excuses that are likely to inhibit productivity in your enterprise.

Question: "What do you think are the major reasons that salespeople fail to close sales?" Follow-up: "Which of those reasons do you see as a problem for yourself, and how would you handle those problems selling our products and services?"

Interpretation: Listen for out-of-balance emotional needs in the answer. People with low sales initiative will be uncertain about how to solve the problems, or their solutions will be unrealistic.

High-sales-initiative candidates will possess an eagerness to answer this question and will respond with action-oriented ideas about freeing up salespeople to sell. Experienced reps with high sales initiative tend to complain about the organization erecting barriers to contact initiation (too many meetings, too much paperwork, etc.). Applicants with low sales initiative are more likely to find something to blame for poor performance (high prices, poor marketing, out-of-touch managers, etc.).

Watch body language and listen for sighs of resignation or any defensiveness.

Question: "How many sales appointments did you have daily or weekly?"

Interpretation: Another strong indicator of sales initiative in veteran salespeople would be their appointment calendar. Candidates with low sales initiative don't have as many appointments.

Watch body language and listen for excuses. Excuse making is the hallmark of poor sales initiative.

OUT-OF-BALANCE APPROVAL NEED

Definition: Top producers possess accurate empathy. They are sensitive to the give and take of relationships without becoming either overly agreeable or close avoidant. This requires a balanced emotional need for approval. Too little and a rep may be overly oppositional; too much and your candidate may be unnecessarily accommodating.

How to Spot the Problem:
Empathizing behaviors are extremely difficult to spot and are easily overlooked in the typical employment interview. Candidates are on their best behavior and tend to be more compliant than usual. Empathizers, however, never turn off the need for approval. They come across as genuinely nice people. You can't help but like them. On the other extreme, approval-avoidant individuals can be spotted using many of the same questions developed for the out-of-balance control needs.

One telltale behavior of empathizers is that they send many positive visual cues to you when you are speaking. For example, they are likely to nod their head yes in agreement with almost anything you say, even if it's something negative. Empathizers establish rapport quickly, which makes them very attractive to sales recruiters, especially if the company's sales process is built around consultative or relational approaches to selling. They are adept at telling you exactly what you want to hear. It takes a skilled and disciplined recruiter to spot someone who is too agreeable, too understanding, and too nice; it is even more difficult to apply the unique behavioral-interviewing skills necessary to uncover the approval-driven salesperson. Why? Because the empathizer will tell you what you want to hear. They do this intuitively. Some behavioral-interview questions are as follows.

Question: "What kind of manager do you prefer to work with?"

Interpretation: Listen for strong people themes, such as teamwork or customer service. If your candidate mentions an appreciation for a manager who is appreciative and understanding, you may be listening to an empathizer give expression to a need for approval.

One check for empathizer tendencies is to not give any positive feedback as the rep speaks. Remain stone-faced. Full-blown empathizers will sense your aloofness and begin adjusting their comments in an effort to gain your approval. Listen for apologies or shifts in logic or emphasis.

Question:	"What was your biggest pet peeve on your last job?"
Interpretation:	Typically empathizers will deny any problems initially. They may appear almost naïve in their assessment of conflict or trouble. If problems are denied, follow up by inviting the empathizer to open up. Say something like, "Oh, come on. It's just you and me." Or, "I'm not going to tell anyone." One fault empathizers have that undermines sales organizations (in addition to not being able to close sales) is that they are terrible gossips. Watch body language and listen for a change in voice inflection that becomes whining or passively aggressive followed almost immediately by an apologetic demeanor.
Question:	Ask the candidate to sell you your pen or pad of paper (anything on your desk). Shake your head no during the presentation. Give no positive feedback. Then look at the candidate and say, "I'm not sure you have what it takes to be successful here."
Interpretation:	Empathizers will back down easily when confronted with anything less than glowing approval. Does the candidate attempt to overcome your objection or does he give up? Could you afford this behavior if your customers and prospects raised objections? Salespeople with out-of-balance approval needs let the customer control the sales process. They are quick to

accept objections and usually wait for the customer to tell them they are ready to buy.

Watch the body language for signs of undue stress or uncertainty. Listen for subtle shifts in the logic or direction of the sales presentation as the salesperson tries to intuit your likes and dislikes.

OUT-OF-BALANCE CONTROL NEED

Definition: Selling requires persuasion and determination. Successful reps, therefore, must possess a balanced emotional need for control. Too little and a rep will be overly deferential; too much and your candidate may be unnecessarily confrontational or oppositional.

How to Spot the Problem:

Controller behaviors are spotted with your eyes and ears. Visually, look at your candidate's face. An out-of-balance control need is frequently reflected in an inability to smile naturally. Controllers smirk. When you talk, their eyes focus intently on you and seldom move. This gives the appearance that they are careful listeners. They do listen well, not for the sake of relating, but to find a weakness to exploit or to gain a competitive advantage.

When they talk, controllers speak in short, forceful bursts, punctuating their statements with finger stabs or other aggressive gestures. Although it is more socially acceptable for men, women, too, may display assertive, dominant behaviors. Review these behavioral-interview questions, which are designed to validate the hypothesis that you are dealing with a controller.

Question: "What kind of manager do you prefer to work with?"

Interpretation: Listen for themes of loyalty and respect. These are aspects of leadership critically important to controllers. If your candidate mentions a preference for a manager who doesn't require a lot of teamwork or collaboration, you may be listening to a controller, who typically prefers to work alone.

Watch body language for shrugs and other gestures that minimize the importance of the question. For the controller, the best thing a manager can do is get out of his or her way.

Question: "What was your biggest pet peeve on your last job?"

Interpretation: Control-oriented individuals should be quick to respond to this question, as they can often be critical and fault finding. Listen for a need to criticize those in power. Will the pet peeve likely resurface in your organization? How is this applicant likely to respond to your efforts to coach or manage?

Take special notice of any themes that deal with difficulty accepting change. Controllers resist change and are likely to demand solutions to complex problems by returning to outdated, traditional responses. They are notoriously suspicious of computers or anything else that makes them rely on anything or anyone other than themselves.

Watch body language and listen for signals of someone who doesn't do well in situations that demand flexibility or change.

Question: Ask the candidate to sell you your pen or pad of paper (anything on your desk). Stop him after a few minutes and aggressively disagree with the approach or criticize him for something said.

Interpretation: How does the candidate respond to criticism? Would this response be appropriate with your clients? Salespeople with out-of-balance control needs may become belligerent and argumentative. If the control need is balanced, the individual should accept coaching and adapt the sales approach to the new selling situation.

Watch the body language and listen for whining complaints or defensive criticism.

FOCUS

Definition: Focus is the ability to set and keep production priorities without becoming distracted by competing interests or goals. Focus is a critical asset in direct sales but can be a liability in situations that require salespeople to multitask. Extremely focused individuals will be frustrated in organizations that flit back and forth between sales approaches or continually tinker with the sales process or product lines. The more multitasking is important to your sales efforts, the less critical focus may be to productivity.

Focus is a problem for two types of people:

1. Salespeople who are being stretched in many different directions from competing personal priorities, such as working single parents
2. Individuals who may suffer from attention deficit disorder or who require more outside stimulation that most people

How to Spot the Problem:
This productivity barrier is difficult to detect in a discussion with a candidate because a job interview is special. Interviewees know the priority of doing well and paying attention to everything that is said. Focus problems typically don't show up until later, when the rep settles into the routine of the job and finds he has become quickly bored or she is distracted by outside interests. Low-focus salespeople may be restless during the interview or have difficulty concentrating on the topic of discussion. They may frequently feel overwhelmed with their own busyness. A few may acknowledge they have a problem setting priorities or saying no to the many worthwhile requests to their time and attention. If keeping focus is important to your sales position, here

are some sample behavioral-interview questions around that critical topic.

Question: "What do you like to do in your spare time?"

Interpretation: Does the candidate joke or complain about not having any spare time? This is typical of low-focus individuals. Follow up by asking about some of the activities that keep the applicant busy.

If you hear a litany of interests and demands, do any pose conflicts with career? For example, a candidate dedicated to coaching Little League may not work out selling life insurance or other consumer-type products that require extensive night and weekend work.

Watch the body language and listen for signals of someone who can't stand being bored.

Question: "Have you ever had so many things going at once that you unintentionally scheduled different activities at the same time? How did you handle that?"

Interpretation: Low-focus individuals do this often. With so many activities and interests competing for their energy, they can easily become confused.

Does your low-focus candidate have a strategy for dealing with the need to overcommit, or does the applicant feel overwhelmed and victimized by busyness?

Don't confuse low focus with being disorganized. Many people who are easily distracted have learned to cope with their low focus by meticulous orderliness.

Watch the body language and listen for signals of someone who is easily distracted.

Question: "How have you maintained focus in the past concerning your daily priorities and longer-term goals?"

"Tell me about a time when you exhibited strong focus in managing your priorities."

Interpretation: Low-focus individuals may have difficulty with this question. They may ask you to clarify for them.

Does the individual have a strategy for dealing with the situation of a company or manager who burdens the team with unproductive activities (excessive reporting, meetings during peak sales time, etc.)?

Watch the body language and listen for signals of someone who is easily distracted.

TELEPHONE SELLING

Definition: Impaired telephone selling can be a very expensive problem that impacts productivity in direct sales. Obviously, it is the highest-ranking cause of failure for inside salespeople. If using the telephone to sell or set sales appointments is not important to your marketing efforts, you can safely ignore this form of contact hesitation. If you are recruiting to a phone center job, having no emotional barriers to telephone prospecting surely would move to the top of the list.

Impaired telephone selling is a productivity barrier characterized by discomfort with making prospecting telephone calls or using the phone for any sales-oriented calls. Individuals with impaired telephone-selling skills would rather contact individuals face-to-face than use the phone and, in severe cases, develop what can only be described as a phone phobia. They have no difficulty using the telephone to make a doctor's appointment or to order a pizza, but if asked to make prospecting phone calls, they hesitate and often show physical signs of stress (pacing, heart palpitations, etc.).

In recent years do-not-call lists have greatly curtailed the degree of telemarketing calls. This has not lessened the problem of telephone contact hesitation but has increased it. Salespeople may be treated more rudely if they call someone who has asked to be left alone to prospecting efforts. Do-not-call lists have made reps more hesitant to make telephone cold calls to private individuals who do not have a relationship to the company.

How to Spot the Problem:

Contact-technology issues can only be discovered in an interview by asking questions specific to that type of prospecting or client contact. For inside sales jobs, you could require the candidate to call you several times and conduct initial job interviews over the phone. Not only does this weed out the individuals who may hesitate to pick up the phone to initiate conversations, but it can also allow you to gauge the phone presence of the prospective telesales representative.

Ask the following questions only if using the telephone is important to promoting your product or service.

Question:	"Tell me about how you used the phone in your last job. How many sales telephone calls did you make a week? Did you prospect on the phone or use it in some other way?"
Interpretation:	Does the aspiring salesperson react to this question in any emotional or stressful way? Listen to the priority given to phone prospecting in the candidate's experience. Follow up more assertively if the candidate was attracted to a previous sales job because appointments were preset by others.
	Is the level of phone activity reported by the applicant acceptable? Will your contact activity mean a significant increase in phone activity?
	Watch the body language and listen for excuses.
Question:	If the phone will be used to make cold calls to consumers, bring up the subject of annoying telemarketing calls that we all get at home. Ask, "How do you handle those kinds of calls when you get them?"

Interpretation: If the interviewee invests a lot of emotion telling you how awful and intrusive these calls are, chances are good she doesn't want to be viewed by others in the same way. If a certain behavior goes against someone's image of himself or herself, the individual is not going to want to exhibit it.

A candidate who asks for information about your telemarketing approach is not necessarily suffering from impaired telephone-selling skills. They may simply be comparing your approach to one they already know.

Watch the body language and listen for hesitation or other signs of discomfort or an inappropriate enthusiasm for using the phone. Some phone phobics overcompensate by lapsing into flights of fanciful positive thinking in hopes of throwing recruiters off the trail of their contact hesitation.

OUT-OF-BALANCE ATTENTION NEED

Definition: Top producers are socially outgoing. They enjoy striking up a conversation with just about anyone. Promoting themselves and what they do seems to come naturally to them. In our research it is clear that these people are driven by an emotional need for attention. If that need is underwhelming, a rep becomes shy and uncomfortable with promotion; too much and sales productivity becomes the victim of such vanity that the customer may be reduced to a passive spectator, as the performer talks and talks, listens little, and finds prospecting unprofessional.

This productivity barrier is more costly in strategic selling than in direct sales. Performers do poorly in any sales cycle that requires patience and problem-solving skills. They are usually impatient with details and prefer an intuitive just-do-it approach to handling predicaments.

How to Spot the Problem:
This out-of-balance attention need is the easiest to spot. Although most

candidates show up to a job interview nicely dressed, performers are in a special category of fashion savoir faire. Their motto is "dress to impress." There's nothing wrong with a professional appearance, but for performers, the clothes they wear, the kind of watch they own, the jewelry they flash, and the car they drive are extensions of themselves. They overidentify with the symbols of success. To the performer, success is a look, not necessarily something rooted in performance.

Their business cards may introduce them with hyphenated last names and initials in place of a first name. They put their pictures everywhere they can: on business cards, on résumés, on signs. Another way to quick-spot performers is the signature. They sign their names in huge scrawling letters with lots of flourishes, perhaps to the point of being illegible. Everything they do screams, "Look at me!"

In addition to the visual packaging, performers may also give themselves away by how they talk. They speak louder than most people and are likely to dominate conversations. It's not unusual after the first question for the recruiter to struggle to get a word in edgewise. Performers interview themselves.

Their laugh tends to be boisterous and unrestrained. Performers have a story or joke for almost any occasion. They typically delight in sharing these with broad gestures and dramatic voice inflections. They may affect an accent or have developed some unique pronunciation of a word or turn of phrase, all designed to grab attention. If it's necessary to ask behavioral-interview questions to verify one's performer style, here are some you can try.

Question: Compliment the candidate on his or her appearance or ask about one the obvious success symbols they've worn to the interview (watch, jewelry, fountain pen, etc.).

Interpretation: The more out of balance the attention need, the more the applicant will talk about the item; where it was purchased, the comments it prompts from admirers, where you can buy it, what it means, and much more.

Notice the amount of personal identity invested in the object.

As with empathizers, you can gauge performer tendencies by not giving any positive feedback as the applicant entertains you. Remain stone-faced. The performer may become rattled and even more histrionic in trying to engage you. He may even joke about your denseness. Would this individual get enough recognition in your company? Would the interviewee's ability to improvise be a plus or a minus in your sales presentation? What if someone didn't appreciate the jokes and humor?

Question: "What are some skills where you need improvement as a salesperson?" Or, for someone with no sales experience, "What do you think would be a weakness if you were hired?"

Interpretation: Performers have a difficult time identifying any areas of improvement in themselves. They will either dismiss the question or answer it in a very superficial way. They may admit to impatience but then will quickly turn it around to be a positive attribute. Does the candidate have any insight into his poor listening skills? Will your training be wasted on someone who is convinced he has achieved sales perfection?

Watch body language for minute signs of stress as the performer is forced to come to terms with being something less than perfect.

Question: Ask the candidate to sell you your pen or pad of paper (anything on your desk). Shake your head no during the presentation. Give no positive feedback. Then, look at the candidate and say softly, "I'm not sure you have what it takes to be successful here."

Interpretation: Performers are not even likely to hear what you said and may ask you to repeat yourself. They are experts at tuning out what they don't want to hear.

Performers will become defensive and not hesitate to argue with your assessment of their ability. Unlike more hostile controllers, performers are more likely to respond to your objection at first with a joke or an exaggerated expression of surprise or disappointment.

Watch the body language for clues that the candidate is feeling defensive; for example, pulling back, covering up, or facial expressions of skepticism. The performer is frequently more interested in rescuing a bruised ego than in improving performance.

OUT-OF-BALANCE INFORMATION NEED

Definition: Salespeople must plan and organize their work but not become overly compulsive or perfectionists. When the individual's emotional need for information is out of balance on the low end, the behavior is nearly identical to that of the performer described above. When the need for data is too strong, salespeople become bogged down in the paralysis of analysis. A simple typo or an incorrect figure will cause the high-information-need salesperson to cancel an appointment until the report is fixed. Top reps do not allow the lack of information to deter them from initiating the contact and getting the information they need. Analyzers with excessive data dependency become perfectionists who unnecessarily slow down the sales cycle and bore customers with their endless fact finding or recitation of details.

Our research leads us to believe that the need for information is the least costly of all five emotional needs. In studies done with many high-tech firms and financial-services companies, analyzers are usually ranked among some of the best salespeople. One reason may be the increasingly technological sophistication of the sales profession today as compared to a generation ago. The information age requires that

salespeople comprehend more complex global and market forces than
ever before.

How to Spot the Problem:
Look for someone who is detailed and precise. A good source of clues
will be an analyzer's résumé. Look for it to be both neat and filled with
numbers and minutiae. Another telltale sign of analyzer behavior is
the applicant's signature. An analyzer's love of precision is reflected in
a small and neat autograph. In the same way that they overprepare for
sales calls, analyzers frequently come to the interview overly prepared.
It's not unusual for them to bring a briefcase full of notes and reports.
Don't be surprised if your analytical interviewee whips out a notepad
or portable computer and begins taking notes as you describe the
details of the position or talk about the company. Analyzers can't get
enough information. They have a similar problem when asked to give
information. They frequently drone on and on about all the details of
an answer. They assume that most people are like them and want to be
thorough. One behavior common to many analytically oriented people
is the tendency to look up and to the left or right they talk. This sign that
they are thinking, searching for an answer, can become very annoying if
it is persistent. Don't confuse the analyzer's talkativeness with that of the
performer. The difference is in the emotional content. Out-of-balance
information needs make analyzer responses flat, expressionless, and
more likely to focus on giving data rather than communicating feeling.
If you are thinking your candidate might be too much of an analyzer
than your sales position requires, listen to responses to these behavioral-
interview questions.

Question: "Describe a typical day for me. How do you plan your
                   work?"

Interpretation: Analyzers are likely to be list makers and detailed
                   planners. They typically have strong tendencies to be
                   workaholics. They may cite work as their hobby. While
                   this love of work may seem appealing to recruiters, it
                   doesn't automatically imply higher productivity. In

fact, the analyzer's insatiable appetite for minutiae undermines sales productivity by slowing down the sales cycle and minimizing the number of contacts due to the analyzer's emotional need to be absolutely prepared. Listen to what priority is given to client contact as opposed to getting ready to make the call. Does your candidate seem more interested in organization and tracking information than seeing people?

Watch body language and listen for a monotonous recitation of details. Notice how long it may take for the candidate to formulate an answer. How would your clients and prospects react to this kind of presentation?

Question: Ask the candidate to sell you your pen or pad of paper (anything on your desk).

Interpretation: Analyzers may ask for time to think through their approach. They are uncomfortable when asked to perform spontaneously. Would this response be an asset or liability in your sales environment?

Analyzers will focus almost exclusively on the features of the product they are selling and miss the emotional aspect of the sale. They are more likely to talk about what the product is or does rather than how it will benefit the customer.

Watch the body language and listen for signs of a need to collect, analyze, and recite the facts and figures or all possible options. Are you bored? How will your customers read this presentation?

UP-MARKET SELLING

Definition: Impaired up-market selling can be a very expensive barrier to successful sales performance if your product or service sells to high-income individuals or to the top officers within a company. Individuals with impaired up-market selling skills put certain groups of people off-limits to their prospecting and business-development efforts. In addition to income, some people are uncomfortable around those they consider more educated or culturally refined than themselves. If your niche market does not include marketing to up-market clientele, you may be able to safely ignore this form of contact hesitation.

How to Spot the Problem:
Like all the contact approaches, issues in this particular behavior can only be discovered in an interview by asking questions specific to the behavior. Here are some questions you can ask if up-market clientele are included in your target marketing.

Questions: "What kind of people do you enjoy selling to, and what kind of people do you not like selling to?"
"What, if any, were the target markets of your last sales position?"

Interpretation: Does the candidate put certain people off-limits to prospecting and selling?
Are the candidate's answers appropriate and acceptable?
Watch the body language and listen for excuses.

REFERRAL SELLING

Definition: Impaired referral selling lowers the productivity of salespeople who are uncomfortable asking prospects or existing customers for the names of referrals. They typically believe that asking for the names of their customer's friends and acquaintances could jeopardize the existing sale or embarrass clients. Empathizers frequently develop this impairment. They see lead generation as being unnecessarily assertive and prefer to have the customer volunteer referrals on the basis of excellent service.

The problem here is not a lack of training. Individuals with impaired referral selling know how to ask for referrals. The problem is emotional.

They choke on the question when the time comes in the sales presentation to ask about others who might be interested in the product or service. If your sales presentation requires salespeople to ask for referrals, you dare not overlook this critical skill impairment.

How to Spot the Problem:
Ask the following question if referrals are a necessary aspect of your new-business-generation strategy.

Questions:	"How many referrals were you expected to get from each sale in your last position, and how did you get those referrals?"
Interpretation:	Does the applicant hesitate or raise questions about your request? Hesitation about the issue in your interview is a good indication that the individual will also hesitate to ask for referrals in front of clients. Watch the body language and listen for excuses.
Questions:	"Can you demonstrate for me how you ask for referrals?"
Interpretation:	Does the candidate evidence any training in his or her technique? Does it sound apologetic or confident? Is the act of asking for the referral consistent with the rest of the candidate's self-presentation in the interview, or does this behavior seem unnatural? Watch the body language and listen for excuses.

NETWORKING

Definition: Networking is the ability to mine one's personal sphere of influence for sales opportunities. In consumer sales, where almost everyone is a prospect, networking requires that a salesperson be able to talk to friends and family about what he sells. In business-to-business sales, networking may require the rep to use social occasions to establish business relationships. When this contact technology is impaired, the salesperson hesitates to mix business and friendship. The rep compartmentalizes his personal and professional lives. If networking skills are not important to your sales efforts, you may be able to ignore this contact technology.

How to Spot the Problem:
Ask the following question if you expect your sales reps to network with others in their personal or professional sphere of influence.

Questions: "Everybody has a circle of influence they bring with them to the job. Whom do you know? Who's in your circle of influence?"

Interpretation: Does your aspiring salesperson hesitate to talk about the subject? Does he raise qualifying questions or apologize that he's not at liberty to respond with names? Does your candidate name friends and/or family members in his circle of influence?
Watch the body language and listen for horror stories about failed multilevel marketing schemes or other excuses to avoid opportunities to network.

PRESENTATION SKILLS

Definition: Simply put, this is stage fright. If making sales presentations to groups of people is important to your marketing strategy, you need to uncover this productivity barrier.

How to Spot the Problem:
Simple stage fright is relatively easy to discover. Straightforward questions are best.

Questions: "Tell me about a time when you got up and made a presentation in front of a group of people. How did you prepare? What was the outcome?"

Interpretation:	Can the candidate identify such a situation? Does the subject admit to stage fright? What size group was it? This question may also help you detect analyzers and performers. Analyzer answers should focus on the preparation and fear of looking foolish. Performers, on the other hand, see themselves at their best in front of a group of people. Their only stage fright is when the presentation is over and they have to leave the stage. Watch the body language and listen for hesitation and excuses.

CANVASSING SKILLS

Definition: Canvassing is the ability to comfortably make unannounced cold calls. This contact technology is most critical in door-to-door selling situations. Whether it's door knocking or expecting reps to drop by a prospect's place of business on the way to another appointment, canvassing can contribute to your bottom line.

How to Spot the Problem:
Behavioral-interview questions are necessary to detect emotional barriers to making unannounced cold calls.

Question:	"Have you ever bought something from a door-to-door salesperson?"
Interpretation:	Individuals with impaired canvassing skills tend to see door-to-door sales as demeaning and unprofessional. They may perceive such selling as peddling and are less likely than most people to have purchased something from a door-to-door salesperson. Can the candidate identify such a situation? Do they relate the incident as normative or as an odd experiment? Watch the body language and listen for hesitation and excuses.

Questions: "Can you tell me about a time when you just dropped by unannounced on somebody and tried to get an appointment or sell them something?"

Interpretation: Don't be misled by the words you hear. Can your applicant identify a situation? Does she flinch at the thought of "cold calling" or raise qualifying questions?
Watch body language and listen for hesitation and excuses. Is it possible to succeed in your company without face-to-face cold calling?

CONCLUDING THE SECOND INTERVIEW

These examples can help get you started using behavioral-interview questions. As you gain proficiency in these skills, add your own questions specific to your product, service, or industry. You're looking for the most obvious issues, behaviors that give definite clues upon which you may build your hypotheses. Watch the behaviors you see when certain subjects come up. Hesitation or discomfort with any of these issues does not automatically preclude someone from being a successful salesperson. These behaviors may, however, indicate delays or distractions in reaching optimum levels of sales productivity.

At the conclusion of the second interview, you should be satisfied as to the exact qualifications of the applicant for the job and have determined the degree to which the candidate's skills and experience meet your qualifications.

THIRD INTERVIEW (NINETY MINUTES TO TWO HOURS)

In some cases you may need to schedule a third interview for candidates. For example, you've narrowed your selection to two outstanding choices. Or you may still have questions or concerns about whether a candidate is right for the job. The third interview is a good time to pull in others on the management team. Introduce the candidate to the prospective manager and watch how the manager and candidate interact. Is the chemistry right? Make others on the sales team available for a question-and-answer session or a social function. Later, get together and get feedback on strengths and challenges your current team may have picked up.

Another approach to the third interview is a "ride-with." Ask the serious candidate to accompany you or another salesperson on a series of sales calls. If you use this approach, be sure to give the candidate ample notice and provide a clear dress code (if necessary). Managers should take care to avoid any confidentiality issues with customers. You should also be prepared to provide some compensation if the ride-with will take more than a couple of hours. Finally, make sure your customer understands why a second salesman is along for the ride.

Here are the three priorities for you, the interviewer.

1. Listen. If you're not a good listener, brush up on your active listening skills before beginning your interviews. Successful interviewing doesn't depend as much on asking the right questions as it does on listening to the verbal and nonverbal answers you receive.

2. Watch. This goes along with learning to listen. Be especially alert to visual cues, such as body language and fleeting facial expressions. Don't become so preoccupied with what is said that you miss the more important emotional "tells."

3. Take few notes. Note taking can distract you from listening and cause you to miss important visual clues. It can also make candidates unnecessarily nervous and uncomfortable. Writing down everything someone says can be perceived as an inquisition rather than an interview. Sporadic note taking may also telegraph clues to candidates about the kind of answers you want.

The third interview is to clear up any loose ends and, if everyone involved in the hiring decision is satisfied, making the offer (more about that in the next chapter).

ENDING THE INTERVIEW

This can happen any time in the course of the first, second, or third interview. The longer the candidate has invested in the selection process, the more gracious you will need to be in ending the interview. Here are some common stop signs that tell you it's time to end the interview.

1. You find a major inconsistency in the candidate's employment history or self-presentation. We're not simply talking about honest mistakes. If the applicant has misrepresented himself or herself in any way so as to mislead or cover up a perceived weakness, can you really risk having a person with this character flaw on your team? Be suspicious when a candidate says, "Let me be honest with you." What was the applicant doing previously— lying through his or her teeth? Next!

2. The candidate becomes frustrated, starts to cry, gets angry, or loses his temper with you. Better to see this behavior early on rather than after you hire the oppositional and he or she has created lots of drama on your team. Poor impulse control is a major reason employees are terminated for cause. Although you do not want to unnecessarily provoke any candidate, if you have asked a reasonable question or made a request that you make of all applicants and you get an emotional outburst, it's time to move to the next applicant.

3. The candidate suffers from a bad case of "I strain"—every pronoun is first-person singular: "I," "me," "my," and "mine." This may be a sign of emotional immaturity that could make it very difficult for the salesperson to do what may be best for the customer or other members of the sales team. One interesting technique we've learned to deal with self-absorbed personalities is to ask them to continue the interview without using "I," "me," "mine." This can be a good exercise to test the applicant's creative thinking and problem-solving skills. (The secret to the game is to ask questions.) If they don't get it, time to call it quits.

4. The interviewee expresses hostility toward a previous employer or too quickly assumes the role of victim in describing previous problems. Controllers and performers are likely to be overt in their criticisms of previous managers or companies. Extroverted people tend to blame elements in the environment for poor performance. More introverted analyzers and empathizers are likely to play the victim card and become passive-aggressive about previous problems. They may agree they could have done better but leave the comment up in the air with an unspoken criticism expressed as a disapproving or questioning look. Some employers may deserve a bad reputation, but you need to evaluate how the applicant handles negative feelings in a public environment. Sooner or later something is going to happen that will make the candidate unhappy at your company. You are looking for the emotional maturity in the person to handle negative feelings in a professional way. Wrap up the interview.

5. The candidate uses vulgar expressions, profanity, racial or religious epithets, or improper humor. Again, the assumption is that this behavior is likely to be repeated with your customers. Businesses today are more and more committed to inclusiveness and professional communication in the workplace. Inappropriate language can be a sign of emotional immaturity and an inability to control one's impulses. Of course, once you, the interviewer, introduce coarse language into the relationship, the candidate is likely to perceive this as a kind of bonding behavior, especially among men but not to the exclusion of women.

6. The interviewee demonstrates a consistent pattern of interrupting you. This means that the applicant is a poor listener. The more your sales approach relies on problem solving and determining customer needs, the less effective this candidate is going to be. The inability to listen is associated with increased error rates and poor rapport building. Interrupt the interview.

7. The aspirant manifests annoying habits. He picks his nose. She has an annoying squint when she's thinking. He clears his throat loudly and habitually. She says "uh" and "ya know" before and after nearly every sentence. He sucks his teeth or uses flighty hand gestures. It can be anything, and we've seen all these and many more. If these habits annoy you now, chances are they will annoy your customers, and your annoyance will only grow over time. End the interview.

Practice your let-down speech. It should be a carefully crafted statement. If you get a stop signal early in the first interview, you can do some PR for the company and, as we highlighted earlier, inform the candidate that there are still people to interview and you will be in touch. If the do-not-hire decision is made during the second or third interview, you should compliment the applicant on a strength you've identified that makes him an attractive candidate. Inform him as to when the hiring decision will be made and of the company's policies in notifying applicants.

CONCLUSION

For employment interviews to be effective, managers need to prepare a systematic and objective approach. This chapter supplies the recruiter with sample behavioral-interviewing questions for seventeen behaviors proven to undermine sales productivity. Also provided were interpretations for various answers to those questions. Behavioral interviewing helps avoid asking the three most dangerous types of questions: illegal, hypothetical, and feeling-oriented questions. Stop signs are signals of emotional immaturity, poor impulse control, or inappropriate behavior that mean it's time to stop the interview. The further you are in the interview process, the more gracious you will need to be if your decision is not to hire.

21

MAKING THE OFFER

Now it's time to close the recruitment sale. Unlike other kinds of sales, recruiters don't initiate the close when they see a buying signal. During the course of the typical interview, candidates are likely to give you more buying signals than a blinking blue-light special. Hire Performance demands that recruiters know when the time is right to make the offer. In this chapter we discuss two aspects of making the offer to your candidate: negotiating the package and drawing up the contract.

NEGOTIATING THE PACKAGE

Top salespeople don't stop selling their value to the company simply because the recruiter has made the offer. Because strong sales initiative drives good reps to negotiate for better terms, we think you should be more wary of salespeople who accept your first offer than those who push for more. This will be even more important if your type of selling involves negotiating price or terms. You may want to structure your first offer slightly worse than that for which you are willing to settle. Lower the commission rate or salary. If the candidate accepts it, you've saved some money and you know to begin your training with negotiation skills. If the candidate has the initiative to bargain, you'll have an opportunity to evaluate his or her negotiating abilities. Either way, you can't lose.

EMOTIONAL NEEDS AND NEGOTIATION STYLE

Before looking at some dos and don'ts for professional negotiating, let's look at how the recruiter's emotional needs impact the give-and-take of negotiation. Here are some insights, drawn from research and experience, into how one's behavioral style might predict negotiation strengths and weaknesses.

CONTROLLERS

High-control-need individuals approach negotiation as a war. It's not give-and-take so much as it is attack-and-withdraw. Controllers may perceive negotiation as someone trying to take something away from them, and typically they react by either becoming bullies or adopting a take-it-or-leave-it attitude. The controller brain seems wired on a binary circuit—either it's all on or all off. If they don't attack, they ignore or minimize the importance of the people or issues involved. The implication is that controllers really don't like to negotiate. One controller we know tells applicants who try to negotiate a better deal, "The last applicant who tried to negotiate terms just left, and he was a lot more qualified than you."

Controllers sense the subtle but very real power shift as their role changes during the course of the job interview. Recruiter controllers enjoy playing the part of the interrogator (they like asking questions) but feel at a distinct disadvantage when becoming the supplicant (asking the candidate to accept the job). They fear losing control. To counter these feelings, controllers sometimes employ an interesting strategy: they preface the job offer with a litany of candidate deficiencies. Here's an example. "Well, Bob, even though I'm not sure your background is what I'm looking for and you don't bring near the client base of many I've interviewed, I'm willing to give you a try. But I'm probably cutting my own throat." Minimizing the candidate's talent and potential helps the controller feel superior and more completely in control, seldom realizing that this technique not only undermines teamwork but plants seeds of future disloyalty and a need for retribution in the mentally aggressive candidate.

Controllers can improve their negotiating position by using the strengths of their style (competitive listening skills and strategic decisiveness) to quickly evaluate options and to make constructive contributions to the negotiation process. Effective negotiators realize that they can stay in control and get more of what they want by seeing the offer's strengths and weaknesses from both sides and suggesting alternatives for good decision making.

PERFORMERS

Performers cannot, do not, and will not admit to weakness. They see themselves as good at everything they do, including negotiation. But performers must manage two critical issues if they are to learn the art of the deal: 1) impulsiveness; and 2) impatience. Performers are convinced that they win people over to their side in any negotiation by their charm. Their need for attention can blind them to the relational subtleties and sensitivities required for good negotiation. For example, because they are concerned with how they look and sound, they don't listen well and consequently miss bargaining cues. They become agitated if they think they're not being taken seriously—a serious mental mistake at the negotiating table. The performer's impulsiveness violates a basic principle of good negotiation: be patient while the other side responds. Performers can't stand silence. We have watched a performer recruiter ask a candidate about compensation and seen the candidate start to answer and then pause to think of the right word, only to have the performer finish the sentence for the applicant and compromise her own bargaining position.

Performers can improve their negotiation skills by practicing ahead of time what will be done or said in given situations and then sticking with the script. Performers may need to consult with a controller or analytical team member prior to sitting down at the negotiating table. Performers function best when they engender goodwill in the negotiation, persuading opponents of their commitment to reach a professional and equitable solution.

EMPATHIZERS

The strong emotional need for approval makes it very difficult for many empathizers to negotiate long or hard. The more accommodating their style, the quicker they are to accept initial offers. They may counteroffer but usually only once to estimate the determination of their negotiating partner. One favorite coping tactic of empathizers forced into negotiating situations is to temporarily go over to the other side. Empathizers tell others that they personally understand and would really like to oblige, but the company or their boss or somebody else in a black hat has already made the decision. Empathizers learn to cop out in tough negotiations by playing someone's victim. Empathizers contribute to the negotiation process with their strong listening skills and ability to sense the emotional tone of the conversation. Highly accommodating individuals will likely work best in a supportive role rather than taking the lead in hammering out deals.

ANALYZERS

The patience and detail orientation of analyzers usually make them good negotiators. Because they intuitively remain emotionally aloof from the process, they gain the advantage of objectivity seldom discovered by empathizers, performers, or controllers. However, this composure can also minimize their effectiveness as negotiators if they communicate an uncaring, cold detachment from the process. Analyzers are also less likely to get beyond facts and figures to find the personal motivations of people.

TEN TIPS FOR NEGOTIATING A PAY PLAN

Using emotional needs as the basis for understanding negotiation, here are ten key principles for negotiating the new employee's package.

1. *Never discuss specifics of pay until you're ready to offer the job.* You don't really know how much a candidate is worth until you complete your fact finding. You don't need to shy away from compensation in early conversations, but if the candidate asks about the pay, you could say, "Between X and Y, depending

on skills and experience." Until you are in a position to better assess the candidate's skills and experience, you're not ready to talk money.

Note: It is illegal to ask candidates about the minimum acceptable wage at which they will accept the position. Besides being illegal, it's demeaning and petty.

2. *Don't forget the value of benefits and perks.*
   Benefits can comprise up to 40 percent of a pay plan. Don't overlook the value of insurance, stock options, bonuses, employee discounts, vacation, sick pay, company cars, club memberships, and other amenities when you put together the package. If a candidate lives nearby, that can also count as an indirect benefit, although you should not specifically mention it. If you can't budge on salary or commission, you may find some room to negotiate with benefits and perks.

3. *Always work for win-win outcomes.*
   If it's not a good deal for both you and the candidate, chances are excellent that one of you will eventually bail out of the relationship feeling victimized or angry. Constructing a pay plan that appeals to both you and the applicant calls for creativity and openness more than cleverness and subterfuge. Avoid trying to beat up the other party.

4. *Stay professional and upbeat.*
   Never minimize or demean a candidate, even if you get a stop sign. Threats, ultimatums, and raised voices are indicators that you need to call a break in the negotiation process. Losing your cool gives the other side powerful ammunition that can be used against you, not only in the negotiation but in possible litigation as well. Always avoid getting personal. Keep discussion focused on the job and the opportunity. Avoid negativity. If you must introduce a negative comment, preface it with at least one compliment and raise it as a question (remember the power of CQ).

5. *Avoid unilateral concessions.*
   Don't give up anything without getting something in return. Likewise, don't ask the candidate to give up something without offering a matching concession. Negotiation is a two-way street. Building a winning sales team is impossible if teamwork is undermined at the start of the employment relationship.

6. *My price, your terms, or vice versa.*
   This is a simple, practical way of implementing point number 5. If your candidate draws a line in the sand demanding a specific compensation package, you can stipulate the terms of performance. If you can't negotiate what you pay your salespeople, perhaps you can bend a little on how or when.

7. *Be willing to walk away.*
   If you can't say no, you're simply in no position to be bargaining in the first place.

8. *Mirror a style compatible to that of your candidate; avoid style clashes.*
   In negotiating a pay package, remember to always negotiate from a compatible style. For example, your candidate responds to your offer by saying, "I need to check with (my wife, my family, some friends) before I decide." Mirror this empathizer style by adopting a compatible analyzer style. Enumerate benefits that appeal to the candidate's relational sensitivities. Don't slip into a controller role, because we know empathizers and controllers don't mesh well. So, in the case of negotiating with an empathizer, using a bottom-line, take-it-or-leave-it controller-negotiation tactic would probably prove counterproductive. Similarly, since performers and analyzers don't usually mix, a performer recruiter expecting a snap decision from an analytical candidate may be nonproductive and unrealistic.

9. *When in doubt, ask.*
   Remember, you're inviting someone to join your team. When

you negotiate, be careful not to bargain in ways that undermine teamwork by creating adversarial relationships. When you reach an impasse or stalemate, ask your candidate for help. Honesty really is the best policy in these situations. If you want the candidate on your team but legitimately can't meet a compensation demand, turn it around; ask the candidate to help you brainstorm some options for reaching both your goals. Likewise, if you suspect that a candidate is using some negotiation trick or technique on you, just point it out. "Are you creating a false urgency by telling me you would go to our competitor?" Cleverness is no substitute for integrity in the negotiation process.

10. *Put it in writing.*

The more complicated the negotiations, the more important it will be to commit your agreement to paper. Be careful not to confuse your letter of agreement with a job contract. The KISS theory applies here: Keep It Short and Simple. List whatever you've agreed upon, including compensation, benefits, job title, starting date, and terms of performance reviews. Include the letter as an addendum to the employment contract.

DOCUMENTS

Ask your attorney to provide you with an employment contract that meets the legal requirements of your state or province. Typically, sales recruiters must address at least two legal issues in putting together the employment contract: noncompete agreements and work-for-hire agreements.

NONCOMPETE AGREEMENTS

Turnover is part of the landscape of business. Top salespeople have a way of being discovered by your competitors and moving on. Defectors can not only take your customers; they may also possess strategic information about new products, clients, and pricing strategies—information that could give your competition an unfair advantage. Many businesses attempt to control this risk by including noncompete agreements in their standard employee contract. Noncompete agreements specify that if the salesperson leaves the company, she or he will not accept employment from a competitor or start one's own competitive business within a fixed limited time (usually six months to two years). Noncompete agreements must also specify a limited geographic area, usually a certain distance from the employer's place of business. Noncompete agreements are illegal in some states and may be invalid or severely restricted in others. Your attorney will be able to advise you about regulations in your state.

WORK-FOR-HIRE AGREEMENTS

Work-for-hire agreements give the company legal ownership of all ideas and inventions the employee may generate in the course of doing the job. For example, Gretchen sells widgets for XYZ Company. One day Gretchen gets an idea from a customer for improving the product. She discusses her idea with an engineer who was recently fired from XYZ. The engineer sees the profit potential, forms a partnership with Gretchen, and begins selling the new and improved Turbo-Widgets. XYZ sues Gretchen and the engineer under the work-for-hire clause of their employment contracts. It's possible that if Gretchen and the engineer could prove that they developed the product without any employer resources and that the new product is outside the realm of XYZ's business, their previous employer might have no legal recourse. Again, consult with your attorney regarding the advisability and scope of any work-for-hire agreements that may be necessary in your employment contract.

CONCLUSION

Negotiation skills are essential for building a winning sales team. In this chapter we enumerated the following:

- Stay professional and upbeat, never defensive or petty.

- Always work for win-win outcomes.
- Be willing to walk away.
- Avoid unilateral concessions.
- When in doubt, ask.
- Mirror a style compatible with the emotional needs of the applicant.
- Don't discuss pay specifics until you're willing to offer the job.

Knowing one's behavioral style can yield important insights into negotiation style as well as the bargaining tactics of candidates. Be sure to consult your attorney for any legal documents you may need, including employment contracts and work-for-hire agreements.

22

WE WANT TO TAKE YOU HIRE

We may not have answered every question a recruiter could possibly have in this book, but we wanted to address topics that from our experience should help entrepreneurs, managers, and professional recruiters do a better job at spotting real sales talent and structuring a selection process that doesn't waste time or energy on nonessentials. We believe that the greatest contribution we can make to your recruitment effort is to provide you with a practical model for understanding why people do what they do and some tools for implementing that theory into everyday practice. Our approach is rooted in the science of sales. Don't get bogged down looking for subjective feelings and asking hypothetical questions. We've given you specific behaviors to look for and discussed how those behaviors relate to the overall development of the sales rep in our Four Levels of Sales model.

FOUR LEVELS OF SALES

The Four Levels of Sales model helps you to prioritize the skills and attributes you are looking for in an applicant. Without knowing how salespeople develop, recruiters are left to their own intuitions or the conflicting expectations of hiring authorities who often have no insight into what makes salespeople successful. This leads to recruiting on the basis of impulse and gut feel. The typical interview process makes it seem that how a salesperson talks is the most important aspect of selling. But we know from our research that this isn't so.

Level 1 comes first. Can the salesperson exert enough energy and initiative to get in front of enough prospects and customers every day to meet personal and corporate goals? How the applicant responds to the action line of the ad is primary to anything else. The more contact-dependent the sales job is, the more initiative should be required of the applicant in responding to the job opportunity. Our research demonstrates that this is the most accurate predictor of sales success any recruiter can build into the selection process. Without the energy, the drive to achieve goals, and the initiative to approach opportunities instead of avoiding them, the glib self-confidence of any candidate is a moot point.

Addressing issues at lower levels has the effect of correcting deficiencies in higher levels. For example, clarifying goals at Level 1 makes it easier to focus on priorities, a Level 2 behavior. Addressing risk sensitivity may free up the Level 2 problem-solving abilities of the salesperson. Addressing Level 2 issues of coachability has a direct impact on Level 3, bringing the person's emotional need for control into alignment.

Level 3 builds on the successful achievement of Levels 1 and 2. For example, improving problem solving at Level 2 helps bring into balance the performer's tendency to avoid complexity. The communication style of the best salespeople is usually balanced; that is, no single emotional need dominates the behavior of the rep. This allows the salesperson to adapt his or her personal style to the emotional needs of the customer. Adaptability to different kinds of customers is a more important skill than that the salesperson has a single-minded approach to sales conversations. Barnett's integrated model allows further refinement of the deeper dimensions of compatibility within Level 3 that promote more complex influence strategies by the salesperson. Turns out that there is no one right way to sell except the way the customer in front of you wants to buy.

Bringing our emotional needs into balance enables us to focus on the behaviors that help you exceed expectations and attain the highest levels of productivity and success. We call this Level 4. Level 4 behaviors vary depending on the type of job and the type of selling you do. If prospecting and customer contact is important to productivity, Level 4 is about uncovering approaches to multiple clients simultaneously or to working only warm leads that have a better chance of bringing in new business. In the area of strategic sales, Level 4 looks at one's ability to function well on a team and to move the complex, big-ticket sale through the maze of gatekeepers and multiple decision makers.

RECRUITER'S LEVEL 4 SKILLS

We have shared what we believe are some critical Level 4 skills and behaviors if recruiters are going to exceed expectations and discover Hire Performance. These included:

1. **Leveraging the pay plan.** You need to know how to structure compensation in such a way as to improve productivity rather than to hamper it.

2. **Knowing where to look for qualified candidates.** In an employer's market, job Internet sites can hamper production by overloading the recruiter with minimally qualified applicants to sort through. We recommend developing your own local sources of leads that include your personal network of professionals along with religious and community groups.

3. **Developing a system for handling résumés.** You can't and don't want to read every résumé you receive. You need to develop a system for prioritizing the ones that seem to be the best fit. We suggested a two-step model: the scan sort in which you look for certain key elements and then the deeper dive into the most-qualified candidates' materials, marking up the résumé with compliments and questions.

4. **Using social media appropriately.** Not all social media will be legal or even all that helpful. However, some of the business-oriented networking sites can be helpful in completing the picture of an applicant's work and education history.

5. **Checking references.** This is another Level 4 skill that can be unnecessarily dismissed or overlooked due to the perceived

bias inherent in an applicant's references. We shared a couple of skills for getting more than job title and dates worked.

6. **Interviewing.** An interview is more than mere Q&A. It's a laboratory in which recruiters can test their hypothesis about a candidate. The skilled interviewer is not only listening to what the applicant says but is watching to see if there is congruity between words and actions. We supplied behavioral-interviewing questions and interpretations for seventeen key components of Hire Performance in a three-interview selection process.

7. **Using assessments.** Since this is our specific field of expertise, we spent quite a bit of time trying to help you become a more educated consumer of employment tests. In addition to telling you about the two different kinds of tests (personality and behavioral) we supplied specific criteria for selecting any preemployment assessment tool. Although few recruiters actually go over assessment results with their applicants, we did provide some help on how managers and entrepreneurs who might have an ongoing relationship with the new hire can debrief assessment findings in a positive way.

8. **Making the offer.** Building on Level 3, we looked at how emotional needs impact negotiation skills and offered ten suggestions for negotiating the deal.

Not every skill we've talked about will be appropriate to your specific recruiting task. But we hope you will be able to use some of what we've written to add to your efficiency and effectiveness as a recruiter. Our work may serve as a foundation upon which you can build within the unique policies and procedures of your company. Or perhaps we've filled in a gap in your knowledge or experience that has proven helpful. If you follow the approach laid down in this book, you will have already begun to build the foundations of a mentoring relationship from the second interview. If you don't expect to work with the new hire every day, you can still derive the satisfaction that you have positively influenced that individual's life, enriched your company, and developed your own skill and personal satisfaction. And isn't that the best you can ask of any job?